Ereimagining place
ECOTONE

VOLUME 1, NUMBER 2
WINTER/SPRING 2006

editor-in-chief
DAVID GESSNER

advisory board
BARBARA BRANNON
MARK COX
PHILIP GERARD
SARAH MESSER
ROBERT SIEGEL
MICHAEL WHITE

editors
NINA DE GRAMONT, fiction
SALLY SMITS, poetry
JAY VARNER, nonfiction

managing editor
BRYAN SANDALA

copyeditors
JENNIFER CARLYLE
EMILY GORMAN-FANCY
DAN LEE

designer
EMILY SMITH

editorial staff
XHENET ALIU, PAT BJORKLUND, DOUGLAS CUTTING,
LAUREN BREEDEN HODGES, KIRSTEN HOLMSTEDT,
ASHLEY HUDSON, BETH JAMES, SARAH LONGWORTH,
CHRIS MALPASS, PAMELA MCNEIL, JANIE MILLER,
SUMANTH PRABHAKER, LINDSEY RONFELDT

D0792894

Ecotone: Reimagining Place (ISSN 1553-1775) is published twice yearly by the Department of Creative Writing and the Publishing Laboratory at the University of North Carolina Wilmington. We are grateful for funding from the UNCW Student Government Association and the UNCW Department of Creative Writing. Special thanks is due to Harvest Moon restaurant and the SimmonsWright Gallery in Wilmington. Subscriptions: $18 (one year, two issues). Single copies and institutional subscriptions are also available.

Please address all correspondence to *Ecotone: Reimagining Place*, Department of Creative Writing, University of North Carolina Wilmington, 601 South College Road, Wilmington, NC 28403-3297. Visit us online at www.uncw.edu/ecotone.

On the cover: a portion of *Escape Artist* by Barbara Fisher. Mixed media. 24"x30".

Paintings by Barbara Fisher appearing on pages 45-52.
Beneath the Surface. Mixed media painting. 24"x30".
My Soul to Take. Mixed media painting. 24"x40".
Night Vision. Mixed media painting. 12"x24".
Before I Wake. Mixed media painting. 24"x40".
A Home Away from Home II. Mixed media painting. 24"x40".
Silent Conversation. Mixed media painting. 24"x36".
Precarious Promise. Mixed media painting. 36"x48".
Holding the World Together. Mixed media painting. 24"x30".

ISBN 0-9719308-5-6

Printed in U.S.A.
at Thomson-Shore, Inc., Dexter, Michigan.

UNCW
CREATIVE WRITING

ecotone \ē'kə-tōn'\ n:

a transitional zone between two communities, containing the characteristic species of each; a place of danger or opportunity; a testing ground.

eco Greek oik-os, house, dwelling + *tone* tonos, tension.

WE ARE GRATEFUL FOR SUPPORT
FROM THE FOLLOWING DONORS:

JOAN H. GILLINGS
FOUNDING BENEFACTOR

DIANE BRANN
BENEFACTOR

JOIN THE FRIENDS OF *ECOTONE*

$5000   FOUNDING BENEFACTOR
Lifetime subscription

$2000   BENEFACTOR
Five-year subscription

$1000   PATRON
Three-year subscription

$500   SPONSOR
Two-year subscription

$200   FRIEND
One-year subscription

DONATIONS ARE TAX-DEDUCTIBLE.

Contents

creative nonfiction

fiction

poetry

coda: a migration trilogy

the ecotone interview

art

notes on contributors

On Migration
FROM THE EDITOR

Ecotones are the edges of overlapping ecosystems, places that aren't quite one thing or another. But as well as physical ecotones, there are also temporal ones, times of year when everything is becoming something else, when any sense of permanence, never much more than illusory to begin with, is even more fleeting, and when transience is the norm. The most obvious of these temporal ecotones, what the writer Scott Weidensaul calls "the great pivot points of the year," are fall and spring, the times of the mass bird migrations. Then the world is in movement, almost every winged thing heading somewhere else. These are the times of great unsettling, biannual disruptions, and urgency fills the air. Though the fall migration is driven by a quest for food, not an escape from cold, the birds must race the weather south while simultaneously avoiding the great tropical storms. In the spring they are prodded by the pressure to breed, to get back to home nesting grounds so the work of procreation can begin and so the young can earn their wings in time to begin the fall migration all over again.

This past September I followed migrating birds, ospreys, from my former home on Cape Cod down the East Coast to my present home in North Carolina, then flew after them to Cuba to watch their dramatic and ancient migration through the mountains of that country. Ospreys are large, nearly eagle-sized raptors with six-foot wingspans, known for their swashbuckling dives for fish, and distinguished by their dark masks and vivid black-and-white wing patterns. In late winter, just as the spring solstice was approaching and the ospreys were beginning to stir, I flew down to their wintering grounds in Venezuela before accompanying them north through Florida, up the East Coast, and back to Cape Cod. The trip was, among other things, a different way to see the year. Not merely as days on the calendar, but as a journey along seasonal edges. Of course for the birds this eight-thousand-mile round trip is no "adventure": eight out of ten young birds will not survive. But the ones who do will follow the same route again and again throughout their lives. Each will become an annual Ulysses, making these epic journeys with regularity, leaving every year in mid-September and returning in late March. They will cycle through their years.

I first got to know ospreys when I lived by their nests on Cape Cod. At the time they seemed the perfect embodiment of my own urge to root, to nest, to find a forever place on earth. Ospreys are fanatically committed to their large, sloppy nests, and though the birds are said to mate for life, most ornithologists believe that it is the commitment to the nest, not the mate, that keeps pairs together. It was this commitment to their homes that first attracted me to the birds as I got to know them during their summer nesting seasons. I believed that I, too, had imprinted my home place and would never leave. In fact, I had written a book about the place, about the ospreys, that ended in precisely that way, with my promising to "commit forever to Cape Cod." What happened next was kind of funny, and consistent, in my experience, with what always happens when you make those types of grand pronouncements. Some professors at a university in the South read the book and liked it, especially the fancy lines about how I would never leave, and so they asked me to come teach at their school. All my high-flown yapping about loving and committing forever had been nice, but we were expecting a child and they were offering a salary and health insurance. In the end it was an easy decision. I moved for the same reason birds migrate South: to feed myself and my family.

After my first year in the South I briefly returned to Cape Cod during early July. This time I had no illusions about settling there "forever"—I was now a visitor, a tourist. My first morning I hiked out to one of the old nests, a sprawling unkempt nest that my then one-year-old daughter could have fit quite comfortably in. But she wasn't up in the nest; instead it was filled with other children, three dark brown and white juvenile birds whose insistent cries for food sounded like yearning distilled. These youngsters would imprint this place, the place they were born, and then, in less than three months, they would head out on a daunting journey of thousands of miles to South America. A year and a half later, they would return as adults to this same neighborhood to build their own nests. I still admired the way the birds were drawn to the magnet of home, but I now regarded them differently. After the nestlings had eaten their fish dinner, the oldest and largest of the chicks made his first weak attempts at flight, lifting up like an off-balance helicopter and landing almost instantly. Then, as the bird again lifted and fell, I felt my mind lifting, too, reordering, redefining. It occurred to me that the birds, for all their ferocity in defending their nests, were, like me, only visitors to Cape Cod. After all, wasn't it somewhat presumptuous of me to call Cape Cod "home" to the birds, since they spent less than half the year there? Who knew what the birds considered home? Home might be the South American rainforest where they passed their winter months, or the migration itself, since they lived on the wing for so much of the year. Home might be a place in-between, and this was reassuring to my newly unsettled self.

My old question had been *how to nest*. My new question was *how to be at home in movement*. And it was then and there that I made my decision to follow the birds when they left Cape Cod at summer's end. While before I'd seen these birds as relatively sedentary, as nesters, I now wanted to get to know their other, more flamboyant selves. I wanted to see the year as a journey, a long precarious trip, a cycle of exodus and return. And as a larger experiment in living in-between.

As the editors began to put together the second issue of *Ecotone,* we noticed themes of movement, migration, unsettling. Look closely at Barbara Fisher's beautiful cover and you will see animals, black and white, moving along the edges of a world of lighthouses, ladders, and planets. This it is not a certain world, but a world where, as contributor Jennifer Sinor puts it, "change is the only stability I know." Sinor's piece, "Through the Particular We Come Home," represents well the next generation of place writing. When Wendell Berry returned to Kentucky in the 1960s, he wrote of marrying his native place and proved you could go home again, a radical notion in a country where few have roots. But there are many who, like Sinor, remain wanderers, through circumstance or inclination, and they, too, need to write to place themselves.

But it's hard to root in a shifting world. Ann Darby captures these shifts through multiple points of view in her story about the refusal to accept the certainty of death, while in David Rivard's poems lives spill over into one another through transitions both fluid and abrupt. The themes of being lost resonate in Alison Lester's story of cultural and marital confusion, in the poet Rebecca Aronson's lines—". . . find yourself/nowhere near knowing where you are"—and in the long nighttime ramble of Sebastian Matthews, a ramble over time as well as space (not to mention the rocky terrain of adolescence). Journeys and transformations fill these pages. Burns Ellison take us on an exhilirating trip north to Alaska in the sixties. In "Coachwhip," John Lane sets out in search of stories and snakes, and re-traces his own past as both writer and amateur herpetologist, while in "Cutter," Ben Jones's short story, the protagonist transforms from suburban softie to rugged explorer of his own back yard, newly defined by his fresh scars. Poet Andrew Gottlieb describes a canoe trip that ends "adrift," while Gretchen Steele travels through "a day on the edge/of not being a day" to witness the tragedy of famine.

An entirely different sort of journey is addressed by Margo Tamez in "Béti Leaves," and it is worth noting that the police that guard against these border crossings are called "migras." Brian Laird explores similar turf in a very different fashion, with a grisly and surrealistic tour of the Mexican-American border. Thousands of miles away, in the northeast corner of our country, Robert Root returns to E.B. White's famous lake, and Sheila Kohler's characters undergo a water journey, a trip "between land, in a neutral zone" where ambition bubbles below an amiable surface.

Perhaps nowhere is the thrill of migration so evident as in Derek Sheffield's "Living on James Wright." While ornithologists "open factual arms in dim rooms," it is in the eyes of a thin migrant, a single yellow warbler, that we feel "the breath of fierce light." Luminous imagery fills the poems in this issue: Charlotte Matthews sees "bright specks on the snow" that will soon fly away; Mike White wakes us to "bright hints of deer"; Richard Garcia sees clouds lit up below Taco Bell. Meanwhile, Sara Pennington concludes her "Epistemology of the Fern": "This life is/larger than/anything I will ever know. And smaller." Small, large lives are the focus of the migration trilogy that ends this issue: monarch butterflies annually bloom from trees in Jason Lee Brown's story, while ornithologist Alan Poole lets us follow the miraculous journey of the sanderlings, the familiar toy birds that sprint along the shoreline. We couldn't resist filling out this section with Thoreau's own thoughts on migration and movement, compiled by Jeff Cramer, the Curator of Collections at The Thoreau Institute.

Finally, we would like to thank Rick Bass. Rick's stories provide one of the great examples of nature writing spilling over into fiction.

Ecotone

reimagining place

VOLUME 1, NUMBER 2
WINTER/SPRING 2006

Living on James Wright
DEREK SHEFFIELD

As they aim their laser pens
over charts, ornithologists calmly explain
the slow, sloping descent
of neotropical migrants.
They open factual arms in dim rooms
to show the size of Ohio, puckering widows
and one dirty river become the yardstick
for South America's clear-cuts.

He would catch the yellow warbler
that clutched my hand today, its
song of hurried sweets.
As he broke his lines for the warm
tap of its heart, a hobo
would appear, wearing apologetic smiles,
and a boy with rusty hair,
a real deadeye, sighting
down a gleaming barrel for another
slurred silhouette.

Even the blips of northbound vireos
each spring along the branch between Americas
would cast in his lyric a green wing.
I heard him once, lone Ohioan
opening his throat

three thousand miles
from the gathering outlines
of his state. And when that yellow warbler
lay in my palm, thinned from its journey,

a breath of fierce light searching me
with one dark eye, I stood
as if I did not breathe
and only wind could move me.

Through the Particular We Come Home
Jennifer Sinor

For two years after my youngest brother, Bryan, was born, my father called him George. Come here, George, he would call, holding out his arms to his third child, then running his fingers through Bryan's softly curling hair. It wasn't that my father couldn't remember his name or that there had ever been the chance that Bryan would be a George. Rather my father called him George because, for the first few months of his life, Bryan was struggling to remain alive. Seriously burned over his entire body when a grossly negligent nurse immersed him in scalding water right after his birth, Bryan spent the early part of his life in continual and what can only be imagined as excruciating pain. He lost most of the flesh on the lower half of his body. There was an enormous chance that he would die. Even when it appeared that Bryan would be okay, my dad continued to call him George. As if "George's" loss could be tolerated in ways that the loss of "Bryan" could not. It was only when Bryan, at the age of two, told my dad that his name was not George that my father began calling his son by name.

I have grown numb to the wavelengths below, overwhelmed by the endless blue, bewildered by the thought of waters deep enough to conceal mountain chains. Not since leaving the coast of California five hours ago have we had continent beneath us. Such oceanic dislocation is what makes coming upon the Hawaiian Islands so startling. Land was something we left behind, shed like a wet bathing suit, with the last bits of island clinging to the West Coast. Yet here it is again, quite literally in the middle of nowhere. The most geographically remote place in the world, the islands float, a strand of land pearls, adrift on the Pacific plate. And they appear out my window like a gift.

I love returning to these fragile, impossibly slight islands. I love the way my heart fills when I see them, read them letter-like from left to right: Kauai, then Maui, then Molokai. A familiar alphabet of land arranged on the chalkboard of the sea. Or perhaps I should be more honest here, say that I love the *idea* of my heart filling. I want my heart to fill. Then maybe I would be home.

When I was a child, the cupboards in our kitchen were always full of other people's dry goods. Things my mother never would have bought at the commissary: raspberry Jell-O, dried manicotti shells, unfamiliar brands of baking powder. Refugees from the shelves of neighbors who had recently relocated to military bases in other parts of the country, they always had the feel of the exotic. I would marvel at how my mother would transform the tubes of pasta into something more familiar, slipping the Jell-O into a cake mix without my ever knowing it was there. Slowly the supply would dwindle and with it the memory of the family that had left the goods behind.

In our turn, we, too, would gather the staples that we could not finish before moving and load them into the wagon to carry across the street to other neighbors. Sometimes I wondered if we weren't just circulating the same items: a box of Carnation dried milk, a half-used bag of cornmeal uniting military families stronger than any shared sense of duty.

When you had given away your dry goods, you knew that the end was near. Clean the house for final inspection, a few days in a hotel on TLA and then off to a new state, a new house, a new school. Maybe for this reason I always felt protective of the things our neighbors gave us. Though the items were often unfamiliar to me, I knew what they meant for those who had just given them up. Continually asked to leave things behind, it is amazing how attached you become to salt.

Conscripted at birth and raised in the military, I have never lived any one place longer than five years. Some places I have known only the length of a school year, not even long enough to experience all the seasons. Now, as an adult with no connections to the military and still no long-term commitment to any particular landscape, I have begun to wonder if transience is a pathology, if change is the only stability I know.

Military children are taught to take pride in their ability to recover from loss. They wear relocations like badges, or scars maybe. I remember once interviewing a fifteen-year-old girl, Brianna, about her experience as a military dependent. We met in her living room, underneath a sign on the wall that proclaimed "Home is Wherever the Air Force Sends You." Like most military children, she named moving as the single defining characteristic of being a military dependent, the first thing mentioned and the frame for the ensuing discussion. She began the interview by proudly stating that she had lived in nine places in her fifteen years. Only when the official interview concluded, the tape recorder turned off and the two of us just sitting together, did she confess to me that she "longed for a home." Home, like a secret, lying on the couch between us.

As a new undergraduate at the University of Nebraska, I readily felt my outsider status. In a landlocked state, I was an oddity. My classmates had lived in Nebraska—many in small towns and on farms—for generations. That I was at the University of Nebraska was the result of my not having a home. For the first time I was without family as well. Because my father claimed Nebraska as his home and therefore secured in-state tuition for me, I traveled a thousand miles for a relatively inexpensive education. Military procedure is for the sponsor, most often the father, to retain residency in his "home" state while he and his family move around the country and the world. As my father's daughter, then, I was a resident of the state of Nebraska by default, having never spent more than a week at a time there.

Born and raised in Nebraska, my dad completed his undergraduate degree at the University and then went on to the College of Law. He grew up, not surprisingly, on a farm. His connections to the land are deeply rooted in the soil, the weather, the crops. His parents lived on the land. Several of his brothers still do. It makes sense for my dad to claim Nebraska as his home. He can name the crops that grow there, the streets that used to exist, the farms by original owner. He can shoot carp in the Platte River with the same steady hand and the same rifle that he used to shoot carp when he was ten. The landscape—the openness—fit my father. His desire to save money, his ability to repair almost any machine, his practical and conservative nature grow from the land which raised him, the land which resides in him. These attributes do not grow in me. I poached on my father's connection to the land in order to afford a college education. I passed as a resident. I was a fraud. Without a real home, home became defined—at least legally—as a state in which I could not even tell soy from alfalfa.

~

What happens to the child without a home, the child whose duty has been to leave home after home as part of a culture whose purpose is the constant preparation for the possibility of war? Scott Russell Sanders writes that "if you are not yourself *placed*, then you wander the world like a sightseer, a collector of sensations, with no gauge for measuring what you see." Does that make me a tourist in my own life, gaugeless and empty? And I ask these questions because at the age of thirty-two, having returned to the Hawaiian Islands after a six year absence, having flown across the Pacific in hopes of finding my home, and feeling at first the slight flutterings of recognition when the islands came into view, I discover that not only does my heart remain mute, limp, and unresponsive in my chest when I near the islands, but I also cannot, and this is where the familiar ache begins, where fraud bubbles to the surface, I cannot, face pressed to the oval window of the plane, even tell Michael, my husband, who occupies the seat beside me, which of the islands below is Oahu. I cannot tell him which of these floating masses is my "home." And landing on the runway, my "home" determined by the plane rather than my heart, I feel vacant, empty, like a house once the movers have packed you out. It is an emptiness I know well. It is a vacancy that has continually usurped the landscape, the sense of place, within.

On the first day back on the islands, Michael and I head to the north-shore to my favorite beach, Waimea. As we drive over the island, I gather familiar bits of scenery like seashells. To myself, I recall where exit ramps lead, which stores are where, and when the pineapple fields will come into view. These bits I cup in my hands, run my fingers through, remember. I find comfort in that which hasn't changed. True, the sugarcane fields are now filled with coffee plants and there is a new road that routes cars around Haliewa Town rather than through it, but the land mostly remains the same. I don't take any wrong turns. I get off at the right exit and the panic of the previous day—of not being able to discern my "home" from the plane—slowly begins to subside. I begin harboring the thought, the hope, once again, that maybe this island is my home.

The urgency I have been feeling since we landed yesterday has become compounded by the fact that I have discovered that not only can I not recognize my home, I cannot even name it. Earlier in the morning, Michael and I took a walk to the beach. Along the way, he asked about the birds we saw, the flowers, and the trees. I could name a few—the coconut palm, the hibiscus, the plumeria—but the rest, that little brown bird with the white on its wings, the tiny finch-like birds with gray heads, that pointed peak in the Koolau Mountains, stood familiar but nameless. The very things that companioned me as a child—the bushes I hid in while playing hide-and-seek, the trees I climbed and built in, the birds that squawked at me as I rode my bike to school—remained held in my memory like a smell. I recognized them but could not name them.

Our arrival at Waimea does little to quell my concern. I feel nothing on seeing the bay. Yes, a general sense of awe—Waimea Bay is a beautiful place—but not a sense of home. On the walk to the beach, resigned and empty, I tell Michael that we can sit under the trees when the sun gets too hot. I do not mention that I have no idea what kind of trees they are, even though I have eaten under them many, many times.

The following day I will find myself in the mall near Waikiki, along with all the other tourists, the *malihini*, Hawaiian for foreigners, buying several guidebooks to my "home." I will also buy a map, as later in the day we will get lost and I will no longer be so confident about the exit ramps. These are the roads I have driven hundreds of times. This is the place, the land, I have lived longer than anywhere else in my life. That I buy a map surprises me. That I will use that map unmoors me.

Is it that as a child I did not learn the names of things? Did my parents tell me that we would eat lunch under the Kukui trees at Waimea and I just not listen? Did they explain to me that the plumeria tree, whose flowers we pick to make leis, was originally used to ring graveyards and traditionally the flowers were thought to bring bad luck? Did they name the peaks and the beaches for me? Maybe I have only learned the importance of naming—of honoring—the natural world in later life. Maybe I have only come to realize recently how the particulars of things are the birthplace of both story and memory. While I think this is partially true, my deeper sense is that while I have forgotten much, I was also never told. Not because my parents were preoccupied or selfish, but because as a military family we bore a complicated relationship to the land and, in particular, to naming. In the broadest sense, naming means knowing and knowing brings with it the possibility of grief. And a military family must reduce the number of losses incurred with every move, the number of grieved things. Since you cannot grieve what you do not know you have lost, it is safest not to name. To operate at a level of generality becomes a mechanism of defense. Trees, after all, are everywhere, whereas the Kukui is confined to the tropics.

I was not given names—or more often given the wrong names— because it allowed us, as a family, to remain in charge of the degree of intimacy we had with the land and, ultimately, with a home. We would make up names for everything—for the beaches, for stores, for camp- sites, for people, even for our own pets—and in making up we would not have to really "know." We would not have to fit into a history or a geography that we would only be leaving in a few short months. We would not have to acknowledge that this landscape is different, unique, unlike any other.

When you fear loss, call your son George.

A few days later, driving up the Wainae coast, I name the beaches as Michael and I go along—Electric Beach, Track Beach—and for the first time realize that these names are the names my family gave to them. Electric Beach because it is across from the power plant. Track Beach because you cross railroad tracks to get there. They are our names, not the names the beaches have historically held. They are surely not the names on my newly purchased map. The few names I have for the world around me, for my "home," are hurled into question. I realize that not only can I not name most of my surroundings, but the names I do have are now coming apart.

A few years ago, I came across one of the diaries I kept as a child. In reading the short entries, I was overwhelmed by the homelessness. I never name loss outright, rather it hovers behind the descriptions of friends and daily happenings. On the last page of the diary, the friends I played with during that particular tour of duty come together along with others to form a list of names and addresses. It is my attempt to keep track of those the military has asked I leave behind. Two names appear without addresses: Suzette and Kate. It is not that I do not know where they live. Rather, it is that at the time of this diary I have not left them yet. By recording their names, I prepare literally and emotionally for the fact that in a year or so they, too, will be left behind. They enter both my diary and my life as an inscribed absence.

Cut your losses, shed names like furniture and other heavy items to make weight, host a yard sale, get rid of your dry goods, remain light and mobile because you never know when you will have to leave again. Perhaps it is impossible to cultivate a sense of place when you cannot face the fact that you will lose it, when you must keep your distance to do your duty. Perhaps it is physically impossible for a military child to have a home.

The military builds housing the way it builds an army—uniformly and with the expectation of loss. One set of military quarters is little different from the next, mostly old wooden houses built rapidly for war or the potential of war. No matter in what state you lived, no matter how many times you had moved in a year or in a month, the walls would be the comforting hue of military white, making you feel "at home." The Navy furthered this feeling of familiarity by providing you with regulation military furniture while you waited for your household goods to arrive. Every military family who moved to Hawaii, therefore, spent the first few weeks sleeping on identical beds, eating on identical tables, and watching TV on identical sets.

In three tours in Hawaii, we lived in three different sets of military housing. The first was Hospital Point, an officers' housing area on Pearl Harbor near the site of a hospital that had been destroyed in World War II. To get to our house on the harbor channel, we drove through the Naval shipyard where hulking ships waited in dry docks to be repainted or repaired. Giant gray ships rested naked on oxidized frames, unmasked enlisted sailors dangling on ropes along their sides wielding enormous cans of spray paint and soldering guns.

I remember standing along the mussel-littered shores of the harbor watching the ships move in and out. I was four or five. The sailors in their work blues stretched in long lines of orange life preservers from bow to stern; the submariners stood tasting the last fresh air before diving into the belly of the sea; those on frigates and destroyers soaked in the last images of land. I waited along the channel with my mother or father, guessing the kind of ship, the name, the use, fascinated by how they hid the other side of the harbor only to allow it to reappear as it passed. They appeared as regularly as dinner, bearing guns the size of cars, and left a trail of oil-slicked waves lapping at my feet.

Maloelap, while far from the harbor, was little different from Hospital Point in that all the houses were identical. The interior walls were military white, the floors concrete with soft gray linoleum tiles, and the shrubs grew low and close to the houses. The houses all sat the same way on the street. The lawns the same. The carports the same. The same blue signs hung in the yards identifying the name and rank of each sponsor. In fact, the houses were so similar I once ended up in the bed of my friend's parents, trying to burrow between their bodies, having woken up scared in the middle of the night during a sleepover.

On our third tour we lived in Makalapa, a giant housing community for officers who worked on or near Pearl Harbor. My mother hated it, but like all things in the military we had no choice. We had moved back to Hawaii literally in the space of one week. An admiral wanted my father at the Pacific Fleet Command so we left Virginia two weeks into my junior year of high school. Given the short notice, no housing was available. After we had lived in a Hilton for two months, my mother finally demanded a house. By Thanksgiving, the military had made do by giving us both sides of a duplex in Makalapa. We had two of everything: kitchens, laundry rooms, living rooms. In order to connect the two halves, the men from public works cut holes between the two pantries downstairs and between the two walk-in closets of the upstairs master bedrooms. For years there was no wall between my room and my parents' room. My closet was a thoroughfare; family traffic came through with hardly a knock.

The "g" in government, as in GI (Government Issue), could more truthfully stand for General. For the particular endangers military readiness. An individual, a particular person, is less willing to sacrifice his or her life than is a soldier of the corps. Likewise, it is easy to kill the enemy and much harder to kill a person with a name, a face, a story. The same can be said for military housing. Similarity, the lack of the particular, is a way of life for those in the military, the way to get through life. To regularly exchange one room for another, one kitchen for another, one back yard for another creates stability and community within a system in service to war. We rejected the particular before it could reject us.

Generality comes with a cost, though, one I am only now—more than ten years outside the system—even beginning to understand: the cost of losing the particulars necessary to craft a story. It is through the relationship with the particular, a relationship that like most human relationships is predicated on the possibility of loss, that we come home.

There is a tree that stands near the tennis courts in Maloelap. It is known by those who climb it as The Tennis Court Tree. Wars have been fought over it. Swings made from stolen hoses have been strung from its branches. Boards pounded repeatedly into its limbs to make tree forts. There is no easy way to reach the crotch of The Tennis Court Tree. When I lived in Maloelap, we used the metal casing that covered the thick wires of a nearby telephone pole. You still needed a running start up the pole to make it into the tree. Once up, though, you could scramble the fat limbs like a sidewalk.

Once up, anything was possible.

Here, my friends Karen and Stacy and I would look at the porn magazines that could be found by scouring the nearby bushes where sailors dumped everything from tennis shoes to beer bottles. These magazines held mostly color photos of men, penises hung like forgotten socks across their legs. The stories were about encounters in unexpected places, a van on the side of the road, an aisle in the grocery store. When finished, we would stash the magazines under the tree fort boards or in dresser drawers at home.

Here, we would spend hours playing extravagant make-believe games in and around The Tree. I would kiss Luke Skywalker, swooning against the trunk. Pretend I am kissing Luke. Pretend we are getting married. Pretend we are having a baby. Pretend we are in love.

Here, Stacy swung from the hose-rope and fell—feet bicycling the air—to the ground where she had the wind knocked out of her. It was a terrific and terrifying fall. After she went home, crying and gasping for breath, we wound the hose tighter and tried again.

Here, large toads called buffos lived, Bloody Mary had been seen in the Boydsteins' nearby house, and the gravel was so sharp you had to walk duck-like on the sides of your bare feet to make it to the grass.

Here, we would sit for hours, watching below, waiting for attack, guarding The Tree.

~

A week before I return to Hawaii, I dream that I climb The Tennis Court Tree again. In my dream, I easily lift myself into the arms of the tree. I am not scared, even though I have not climbed a tree in years. I am happy. From its height I can see beyond the fences of the military housing area, over the hill that slopes to Aliamanu school, the hill where my brother Scott first broke his arm, to the bright pinkness of Tripler Hospital, where he was born and where he would later return to have his broken arm set, then out to the ocean, to that magnificent place where you can stand on the edge of continent and contemplate distant lands. From the top of the tree, the edges of the island are visible and known. From the top of the tree, the lines marking military and civilian are surpassed. The borders of both the land and my childhood are noted and then transgressed. From the top of the tree, stories from my childhood rush back to me, reminding me with the incessance of surf how well I know this tree. How happy I am in its branches. How my feet know its limbs, my hands its bark, my heart its height.

I wake with the desire to climb.

I am returning to Maloelap. I exit the freeway and follow Radford Drive around the Navy Exchange. Unlike my drive to the Northshore a few days ago, much has changed here. All the enlisted housing that used to stand smudged with dark red dirt has been replaced by new, windowed, pastel-colored housing that does not even look military as much as it looks like any housing development. At first I think the military has sold this land and that civilians live here now. Only on closer inspection of the front doors do I see the tiny name plates, easily replaced by sliding the plate in and out of the metal bracket when a new family arrives.

Rounding the corner near the driving range of the Navy-Marine Golf Course, I realize with a start that if these houses have been replaced then it is quite possible the houses of Maloelap no longer exist. I drive a little faster while I work over this new idea in my mouth like a piece of hard candy. The houses were old. They could have been demolished. They certainly aren't as showy and new as the replacements I am passing. Heart beating, I accelerate even more.

As I crest the final hill, I see that while the entrance into the housing area has been changed and the road I used to ride my bike on is now covered in grass, the houses themselves, newly painted, are still there. They still sit like flat, square stones on the edge of a shallow hill. I am relieved. I will get to see my old house, number four, and the house where Stacy lived, the hill we used to catamaran down on our skateboards, and the bike path we took to school. They all remain, waiting for me.

It is only then that I wonder for the first time about The Tree.

What I find is that it is gone. There is a large, empty space near the tennis courts where the tree used to stand, but no evidence that it ever lived and grew there. The ground is not disrupted, no roots remain, no stump. I never even knew its name. Space is just space. It is no longer shaped by the sculpture of limb. I cannot readily say just where Stacy pedaled the air.

Like the nearby houses that bear no record of the families that have lived in them, the lives that have been passed within their rooms, nothing gives knowledge that this landscape has suffered loss. Only I know that a tree stood here before. Only I know that Stacy and Jenny and Amy once lived in that once-green house, that Bryan fell from this plumeria tree when he broke his arm, that a stray cat named Gotto had kittens behind a shed that used to stand here. Only I can name the things that have passed, the particulars of the lost.

The pictures I take are pictures of absence, of where the tree used to be. Really the pictures are of an empty, graveled road overrun by grass and weeds. When I develop the roll of film a few weeks later, I will discover my shadow thrown across the ground, an elongated figure holding a camera as if holding her head. Without me to narrate the image, it would appear that someone accidentally pressed the shutter release, the intended subject—a family, a view, event—mere feet away.

Standing in apparent emptiness, a gravel patch marking the memory of what has been left behind, the feeling I have is far from foreign. I am standing in a housing area that I left, surrounded by houses that once held friends who I left, a few miles away from a school that I left, mourning a tree that has left me. In such emptiness, I feel at home.

Space makes us uncomfortable, fearful, vulnerable. We grow trees, hedges, and fences in an effort to create form from space. Emptiness becomes what home is defined against. Kathleen Dean Moore writes that early pioneers would call the experience of empty space "seeing the elephant." She says of their journey: "Starting out, the wide open spaces were glorious—the opportunities, the promise, the prairie, all fused with light streaming down from towering clouds. Then suddenly the clouds became an elephant, a mastodon, and the openness turned ominous.... They saw the elephant and turned their wagons around.... They had to get home." Absence brings fear, and the instinct is to return home to a landscape whose contours, whose particular edges, you can pull close to you like a quilt.

Yet, what remains inside of me is not a landscape but the absence of land, and the particulars I hold are of the lost. In this absence, I define who I am by what I have had to leave behind. There is no other way for me to understand home than through the particulars of passage. I make sense of the world around me by relying on patterns of leave-taking. So when I look at the land, I see what I cannot name and I feel what I have left behind.

To know yourself through absence is not to remain empty. I am the body that carries the tree as well as the friends whose trace is equally erased. I am the one who can tell the stories that resonate with those who passed through rather than with those who remain. In relief to the land is the emptiness that shapes it, the empty spaces between the trees, the air in the hollow bones of bird bodies, the wind in the valleys, the space in the foam left by the waves on the shore. The land holds a place for what has passed through. Like a valley carved by a dried-up river, what has passed can be read as clearly as that which remains. When people talk about the land that defines them, their home, so often it is the particulars of what remains that they recount. For me, it is the particulars of passage that speak most loudly. These spaces, too, have contours. When I look to that land, I see what used to be. The memory of a tree I carry like a suitcase.

Cutter
BEN JONES

Wood is not enough and stone not enough. The house is trembling always, and everywhere John sees rotting, cracking, paint peeling, pipes leaking. If the decay is not apparent, it is because it is hidden and pernicious. He feels panicked, as if the house might fly apart at any moment—nails shoot from wood, the walls shudder with fatigue and collapse. The friction that holds the nails is a poor and pitiful force with gravity and entropy conspiring against it. John walks through the house touching the walls with his fingertips. *Hold fast*, he whispers, *hold fast*.

Mary will be returning from the library board meeting soon. He checks that the boys are both asleep. Roger is six and Oliver will be turning eight in a few weeks. Mary has been planning a party for him—knights, costumes, dragons. She has asked John to clear a bower in the woods, a request he has neglected. He and Mary are both scattered in their energies, as if they could mount one half-decent love between them. He hopes they both avoid the children enough to keep this unevenness hidden from them.

Mary has been put in charge of the library's evening lecture series; the previous month's was a bit of a disaster. The speaker was a poet, widely known by name but little read. He arrived drunk and read without humor a series of poems about jizz and farting. He breathed ponderously through his nostrils. He offered no reflections when he finished, just snapped his book shut, shouldered his coat, and left.

For her the lectures are a vital leavening agent to life so far from the city. They add a civilizing texture without which she would feel that time was moving backward. The women of the board are more focused than Mary on self-betterment. They have traveled little and believe firmly in the idea of progress. They have appointed Mary to find the next speaker with the goal of avoiding the seamy flatness of the jizz poet, and, at the same time, drawing more of the men in town to the lecture. The women present it as a matter of broadening the appeal of the series, but each feels silently that they would like their betterment validated by the interest of men.

When Mary comes in, John pours her a glass of wine.

"They want more men to come," she says. "Do you know any speakers men would be interested in hearing?" John is the editor of a magazine attached to a small art museum; he thinks of his work there as an ongoing attempt to cast light into the darkness, but his job, like everyone else's there, is defined in terms of raising money. The women at the museum all dress in colorful accents and their hair is erratic. They speak urgently about everything, everything is so wonderful, so vital and exhilarating, so breathtakingly unique. Men, generally speaking, hate them all.

"What about Hugh MacPhearson?"

"He's a bore," says Mary. "And he always makes me feel like he's doing us all such a favor." MacPhearson writes a mystery series set in town. He had three or four mildly successful books, but has since written an additional twenty that clog the shelves in the bookstore.

"How about if I make you some dinner?" he says, and retreats to the kitchen. She follows him in and sits silently while he poaches some salmon for her and makes rice and asparagus. She feels spoiled, which she loves, and ticks off for him the board's restrictions for speakers.

"No one political. Not too obscure or pretentious. No self-promoters. Someone from outside of Putnam, but not too famous. Dynamic, but not flashy. Engaging without pandering. No 'storytellers.' The board thinks that men like history, or Russians. What would make Hal come out, do you think?"

Hal is their neighbor. Hal is so utterly Hal that he is difficult to describe. He is in sales, which he relishes. He favors complexly patterned golf shirts and no-iron khakis with loafers; he never seems to wear the same clothes or shoes, yet always looks exactly the same. To John, in his rumpled world, this is some sort of aesthetic miracle. Hal is round, but solid, densely packed. When John heard the space shuttle explosion had been caused by a chunk of foam tearing a hole in the wing, he thought immediately of Hal's stomach, of a chunk flying free and tearing through the side of a car, of Hal like some swarthy Babylonian god, destroying cars by hurtling pieces of his stomach at them.

"Pornography," he says, and she laughs. "Or a professional golfer." He sets her place for her. He has even thought to add a garnish, which he knows will delight her. It does.

"You could get Pettigrew." Pettigrew is an explorer, an old man who cannot remember the names of the rivers he has traveled. He was in the British army after the Second World War, and wrote some books about the desert in the late fifties. "Might be timely."

She eats and he has another drink to keep her company. The evening lapses into a customary silence—when they have run out of conversation about the day and both wish to pass the intimate and fraught conversations of the night unengaged. They read in silence. Mary leaves for bed and John sits in the study, reading a draft of an article written by a graduate student. The writer has described an image of Blake's as procrustean, and John is irked that he cannot remember exactly what it means. The definition in his Webster's is not helpful: "hard, rigid"; he suspects this is as far as the graduate student got, skimming his thesaurus to find appropriately obscure vocabulary.

As he leafs through Bulfinch he can feel his own memory rising to the surface. The robber. The bed. A pleasant, lively dinner leading with gentle, ineffable logic to a walk up the stairs. Sympathetic smiles all around—solicitations of comfort and ease. The iron bed, surrounded by the implements of torture, perhaps a painted flower at the head. The glint of a saw, imperfectly cleaned.

John finishes editing the article. It is not good, but it connects to the needs of the magazine—the prestigious feel of its dense obscurity, the dedicated scholarship of the student, who looks appropriately wan in his photo. John fixes another drink and reads an Italian novel in translation; he wonders if the awkwardness of the prose is poor translation or expert translation of some intentional awkwardness.

His days are marked by textures of reading—newspaper, memos, ponderous emails from the Director, a trade journal, a novel for pleasure at lunch, endless drafts of the new exhibit catalog, print vendor proposals. Without reading or the prospect of it, he becomes anxious. He uses reading to try to change his moods—something heavy like the Italian to make him feel substantial after the queasiness that editing the student article has brought on.

He checks to see that Mary is fully asleep before changing into pajamas she has bought him. He slips into bed, breathing as gently and unobtrusively as he can. He gets under the covers and ceases to move, knowing that sleep will arrive even if he does not settle more comfortably.

Pettigrew is suspicious of the telephone, so Mary has to find him by circling through town for several afternoons. She catches him as he staggers out of the underbrush on a roadside, his woolen socks trailing burrs and flax. He has a groomed mustache and is in that state of healthy old age where he has looked the same for twenty years—craggy but upright, steady on his feet; what comes next is precipitous decline and it will come in a year or two. He assents to speak, provides a list of necessary equipment and their specifications, and then shuffles away.

The library ladies are thrilled. There is much discussion of appropriate refreshments—goat cheese? Tented cakes? Baklava? One confesses, giggling, that she has always thought Baklava is an Austrian winter hat. Another asserts her preference for French rather than Austrian hats, especially for dessert. None of them has actually met a real Austrian. Mary dissuades them from having a themed reading. They agree, but there is further giggling about hat eating and the Austrians.

On the night of his presentation, Pettigrew arrives, shabby but proper, and stands against the wall near the front, waiting for Mary to guide him. People take their seats—an old couple, he already dozing off; the earnest ladies of the board, ramrod straight, filling up the front rows; three divorcees—the smell of white wine and perfume; a lean, intense boy with paint on his hands; and John.

The lights go out and Pettigrew steps forward, the textured light from the projector falling across his face. He shows maps of the Ottoman Empire, the Sudan, Abyssinia, Anatolia; red lines trace the routes of the 3rd Expeditionary Scouts. Pettigrew's narrative consists mostly of dates and supplies, of distances and rations.

"Five men on camels can travel twice as fast as ten men for periods of a month or more. Groups larger than sixty are so slow and difficult to supply that there is no need to engage them militarily; oases will not yield the water to support them and the desert itself will thin them to reasonable numbers. Large-scale attacks are logistical wonders, as they require dozens of small groups to arrive at exactly the same time via different routes, mount their attack, and be able to disperse again before the oases are exhausted."

Then, in grainy black and white: camels, tents anchored in gravelly washes, striking young men with rifles in their laps squinting into the distance; a young Pettigrew, with short hair and a full beard, his cracked lips coated with dust.

"The Bedu are a tribe that trace their lineage directly to Ishmael. They value dignity highly and their own lives not at all. They have no knowledge of medicine or nutrition; they survive by breeding camels and banditry. They freeze in the cold and suffer the heat and hunger and thirst. They believe they live the finest possible lives because the harsh conditions they endure shape them into the strongest, the most noble and the most free men on the earth. They pitied those of us who had the misfortune to live other, more sheltered lives."

John realizes he has never looked at life on these terms before—what shape is his life making him? He has cobbled a life of components— marriage, children, cars, and appropriate clothes, acceptable leisures that let him look at beautiful things and smell beautiful smells, that let his children laugh and not cry—that let them feel safe and loved and never think that the world may end. He has ulcers and spends the odd Saturday on the can shitting bile if he drinks too much coffee or gin. His back hurts, and his heart. At night, his teeth ache. He gets winded on the stairs. He is thirty-eight years old.

Pettigrew shows some slides of British gun emplacements, and a blurry slide of running camels, taken from the air. He talks about the discovery of oil and the disintegration of the Bedu, of the rise of airplanes and the loss of the desert as a refuge.

The lights come up and the ladies struggle to find instructive questions: (Could they improve our scientific methods for breeding cattle? Were the camels treated badly? How did they educate their women?) Pettigrew bears their attention with awkward patience, and leaves.

Mary cleans up the refreshments and John helps to stack the folding chairs.

"Well, what did you think?" asks Mary in the car.

"Very interesting. Especially to think about how long their lives were the same, and how rapidly they have changed. I wonder if they are happier now that they suffer less."

"If they have survived the evils of comfortable clothing and proper medicine? The awful burdens of regular meals?"

He laughs.

"Just imagine the dentistry," he says, and trails off.

John runs the babysitter home; the boys have been good. When he returns, Mary is in bed with a book. He thinks he may give her a kiss goodnight tonight, but she is carefully ensconced. He retreats to the study and tries to read—the Italian, a monograph on Renaissance body art, but the words are vague and stubborn. He sits with his hands trembling, looking for what would be right to read, when he is seized by a startling and necessary idea. He is some minutes with the preparations.

He checks in on Mary and shuts her door gently, waiting after the click to hear if she stirs. He debates turning on the bathroom fan—better to mask his own noise? Or be able to hear if someone is coming downstairs? He turns on the fan. The boys are both asleep. He descends.

In the downstairs bathroom, John lets the blade press against the skin of his forearm—sees it elastic and resistant. He thinks for a moment how remarkable skin is—durable, regenerating, vulnerable. He waits for some sixth grade facts to leap into his mind, how skin is stronger than steel, or would stretch to cover a football field, but none come. He pulls; the knife is sharp—he has sharpened it for this purpose. A short wedge sits white and naked for a moment and then blood wells up. The pain was sharp, but is already indistinct. He makes a second cut, deeper and longer than the first—he is braver now—and then a third. The third is the smallest, but deep. The blood on the knife makes him ashamed and he pushes to finish before he loses his nerve entirely. The blood flows over his arm now, obscuring the cuts. It is brightly, impossibly red, as if it can bear no relation to himself.

He watches a moment longer. The cuts well and the blood runs evenly, not jerking out with the throb of his heart, not a product of his sporadic life. And then he grabs the towel he has made ready (white) and presses it into the cuts. He kneels at the edge of the bathtub and rinses away the excess blood. He daubs at the cuts and then presses down hard to stop the bleeding. He is elated.

In the kitchen, he gets out a gauze pad and tape and hydrogen peroxide. The cuts are still bleeding slightly as he cleans and binds them, but they do not hurt. In fact, his whole being feels charged and alive as he secures the gauze, tears the white tape and draws down his sleeve.

Back in the bathroom, the sight of the bloody knife is shocking and degrading. He feels weak. He throws the towel and the knife into a bag and takes it out to the garage. He scrubs the bathtub, the bathroom floor, the sink in the kitchen. He can feel the indictment of the knife out in the garage. He changes into clean pajamas. The gauze is still blazing white, like a badge of honor for which he has been, in the past, gloriously worthy.

He rises early, before the boys are up. He makes coffee and leaves as quietly as he can.

The supermarket is filled with old people, as if a plague of age has struck in the night and he is one of the resistant few. Even the cashiers are old. The aisles smell of lemony disinfectants or their absence—the chemical idea of what spring might smell like.

He steers to avoid a blockade of women clustered in among the muffins and overhears them complaining. They never complain about the freshness of vegetables, but about the aging fleet of shopping carts. And the answer is not simply new carts, but a new store, or, more appropriately, a NEW STORE. This one is soiled with use (their own). If only it were ten percent larger and shiny—they seem to think that is a good ambition for almost everything in the world.

Looking for towels, he frets about matching the shade of white. He selects a knife, hesitates, then gets two. Planning for his own weakness shames him further. The cutting is no longer an impulse but an activity; it has become a history of deliberate steps and a plan of future degradations.

When he gets home, he finds the house is still quiet. He replaces the towel and the knife, and hides the second knife in the garage. If she finds it there, will it be stranger than if she finds an extra knife in the drawer? He shifts it to the drawer, but wedges it in the top, above the silverware holder, where the chopsticks are, where it might have shifted accidentally. He changes his shirt for a fancier one, and even irons it quickly as he hears stirring upstairs. He makes the boys lunches for school and packs their backpacks. Mary comes down and notices the shirt; she supposes he has put it on for her; it is just the kind of small, formal gesture that feels to her like love. Under his shirt he can feel the tautness of the tape.

Roger comes down, chattering already on the stairs, before he can see them, before he knows anyone is there. Oliver emerges dressed in the same clothes as yesterday. Mary sends him back upstairs. John helps load them in the car amid Roger's bright and breathless talking.

Back in the house, John resolves to clear the bower. He changes his shirt again and, because he has no tools, heads to the hardware store. Putnam's is still a family business—a square-headed father and his square-headed sons, though he cannot remember their names.

In the hardware store the metal—the screws and bolts, bins of nails, chains—all of it shines with the promise of order, of durable building and the knowledges that lie behind it. Plumb. Even the word has a reassuring fullness. The smell of oiled metal makes him think of handguns, of their surprising weight, of their feeling of sufficiency.

He buys gloves and clippers, or loppers as they seem to be called, and a brush saw. Their house, and the houses around it, used to be farms. Stone walls run through the woods where the fields were divided. Maple and oak and birch have grown up, but the forest is still young. The underbrush is dense with honeysuckle and sumac and burdock, and many of the young trees are suffocating under vines.

John begins cutting a few trees and braiding the others into a looping tunnel through the underbrush. He finds a patch of grass and fern under a low-spreading hemlock. He lops some young birches and weaves them into a crude entrance. His cuts ache and sting sharply whenever the brush hits them. Underneath the bandage, however, his arm feels surprisingly strong—he can feel the muscles moving smoothly, responding as he demands of them.

Throughout the day he hears gunshots in the distance at regular intervals—probably a boy with a new rifle, practicing on bottles, or song birds. The boom and echo provides a refrain of violence, of violent acts in the peaceful day, or of the preparations for violence. Men planning for killing, or boys learning to take their place in violent ways of being. He imagines the boy, thrilled to have a real gun—just as John had been—eager to try it out, to see if it could really bring death. To bring death. The gun goes on and on—for an hour, then two—firing faster, then slower, then faster again but pausing, it seems, only long enough to reload. Someone has spent the day shooting. That day, and many others are gone.

He finishes clearing the brush in the late afternoon; he can hear that the boys are back from school. He sits among the ferns and listens to them run and shout. He thinks about sneaking in through the garage, but he stays. The sky is orange, and then purple, and then black. The whine of mosquitoes rises. The boys have gone in, have eaten dinner, are, no doubt, in their beds. He tries to look at the clouds, at the emergent stars, tries to listen to the birds and the insects, to the fall of night, but remains preoccupied with his own discomforts and his endurance of them. The early summer evening is cool; the ground is surprisingly lumpy and scratchy. His shirt is thin and he shivers, twitches as he is bitten.

Without resolving to do so, he reaches a point where it seems necessary to spend the night outside. He imagines if he can fall asleep somehow, despite his discomforts, he will have triumphed over something, over some conception of himself. He tries to watch the stars moving, but they do not. The night seems impossibly long, the compressed hours unfolding in a way that makes him anxious and bored at the same time. He tries to see the shadows changing as the night deepens, tries to imagine the sun on the other side of the world. The night continues without relenting; he does not sleep, at least not as he understands it—he becomes aware and then unaware.

No rain comes, but he can feel the dew well up. The black disappears and the sky becomes light. He is thrilled with the idea that he has survived. He sits waiting for the sunlight to reach him through the tunnel he has made—patient for the world to roll underneath him—all of its seas and shores, all of its mountains. The light strikes his upraised knee and slides down his leg, at once intimate and immense, the sun and earth in service to this moment he has been waiting for. The sun at the horizon accelerates, is up. He rises and returns to the house.

Mary is awake.

"Where were you?" she asks, because she is irritated and because she ought to.

"Out," he says. "I got finished late and was tired. I fell asleep." He tries to make this sound casual, plausible, as if such a thing were even faintly possible.

"There is blood," she says, pointing. The bandage has bled through.

"I know. The locusts, I think, have sharp thorns. They were heavier than I thought."

"Let me help you," she says. He extends his arm like a child. She strips off his dressing. The cuts are no longer bleeding but look fully liquid, as if surface tension is all that is holding back the blood. They look antiseptic—perfectly even, well-spaced, like a contract awaiting signatures. She does not look at him while she rinses them with antiseptic and gently lays down fresh gauze.

"Those are deep," she says. "Are you . . . do you think we should have someone look at them?" What she wants to say is *What have you done? What is happening to you?* She presses down the tape, wishing for each of her movements to transmit in its code: *I am alarmed. You are not who I know.* She lets her hand linger for a moment: *I don't want to understand this. I don't know what is happening.* She looks finally in his face, which is lit and distant. His cheeks are flushed from the heat of the house, from shaking off the dampness of the morning. She feels he is lost, and wonders if he will return, if she would like him to return for reasons other than comfort.

"I'm stiff," he says. "Ground is hard." And he laughs. He turns from her and climbs the stairs.

He likes the look of dirt on his own hands and the smell of the forest on him. He feels like this is a secret he should share with the sleeping boys. He wants to shake them from their beds, from warmth and comfort, put them out in the cold and darkness. They are both curled under their covers, pink and softly peaceful, the work of sleeping past. The boys are ignorant of his impulse to damage them, oblivious to a gaze that is assessing their capacity to suffer, to adapt, to weather hardship and change and deprivation (for the chance at joy, he tells himself, for beauty out from under the glass). He has no desire to hurt them, but feels in this carefully constructed unreality that they are being held back from the world.

He needs to get ready for work, but he wants to hold the smell of the dirt and dew on him for as long as he can. He fills the sink with cold water and dunks his head in, letting the water run over his shoulders and down his back. He does not shave nor shower, but gets dressed in clean clothes. He calls out a cheerful goodbye, to which Mary does not reply.

Sitting at his desk in the afternoon, his arm starts to itch under the bandages. His leafy, earthy smell has faded, overwhelmed by the chemical smells that surround him, of his desk, the carpeting, his clean clothes, that he exudes; he dredges up some splinters from under his nails for the last of the smell of the night. He is weary in the afternoon, but still exhilarated; the world feels endlessly variable, as if any line of action may be considered, any thought arrive, any turn be left or right and every moment charged with what might be done or undone. For a moment, he worries that she has found the knife, and a wave of shame passes through him. Tomorrow, at least, is garbage day, and the knife and towel will be gone.

Mary is going out again that night, still the library—a subcommittee on renovations. He will be careful to be asleep before she returns. She does not mention the cuts.

He buys extra gauze and tape that he keeps in his desk at work. He watches the edges of the scabs grow pale and crumbly—he lifts them off to see a pale white mouth and a deep red throat that wells up. This feeling is as important to him as the cutting. He inflicts the cut, but the healing comes unbidden—does its work without prompting or effort—hidden—automatic; it gathers what it needs without demanding, and the healing happens, finishes, the white line like a signature. It gives him faith that the whole world works this way—that it is inflicted upon, gathers itself and heals. He feels purged for a time, hopeful.

The morning of Oliver's birthday is hot and dry. Mary has made costumes for all eight of the boys who come over. There is a quest for the knights out in the yard and down into the basement, and out to the bower. Somewhere is a dragon, filled with candy.

Mary has dressed John in a tuxedo, which makes him feel festive, although it is nine o'clock on Saturday morning and the sun is glaring in the sky. He has a whiskey and then another. In the bathroom he shakes a handful of Mary's pills out into his hand. He takes two and slides the rest into his pocket. The boys are tearing through the house, roaring and clashing plastic swords against cardboard shields. The cat flees. Mrs. Hendershot asks when the new edition of the magazine will be out, and what exhibits the museum is planning. John ties a balloon and praises Roger's fortifications.

From the yard he can hear Mary's voice, and there is a surprising warmth in it for the children. She loves them, he does not doubt it.

The boys shriek as the dragon comes down and they scrabble for candy. Mary enters, beaming, and John rises to cut the cake. She has made it in the shape of a tower, with a ring of candles along the carefully crenellated edge. Oliver takes in a breath to blow out the candles, but then decides to try to lop off the flames with his sword. He hits the tower near the top. The cake spatters the ring of boys and Mary's face darkens. The boys all laugh, but Oliver has realized his mistake. He gathers pieces of the cake onto a plate and struggles to reassemble them. Mary forces out a laugh and retreats for paper towels. John cuts rough squares. He begins to scoop ice cream onto plates, and the oblivious boys devour them.

Roger cries during the presents, at the sheer injustice of it not being his birthday and for the interminable time until it will be. His cheeks are flushed and grubby and his eyes have an odd flatness to them. The Hendershots leave, then the Wheelers and the Kerrs, and then abruptly everyone is gone. The boys sit calmly watching a movie and there is a small fire in the fireplace.

Mary makes a light dinner, but the boys have been eating candy all afternoon. They trudge up to their baths and into their beds. John rises through his pleasant fog to kiss them goodnight.

Oliver has piled all of his new toys and books onto his bed with him and is touching each one in turn. Today his blessings seem bountiful and he is overwhelmed by them. He settles himself against the mounds of plastic and wood, against the spines of books.

"Tell Mom I'm sorry about the cake," he murmurs. "I just . . . I didn't." His eyelids waver and John kisses him on the forehead to save him from crying.

Roger has thrown himself down on top of his covers. He is wearing pajama bottoms with fire engines on them, but no top. His chest looks impossibly small and frail and he seems to be heaving in his breaths. His face is pinched and damp; he whimpers, not awake but not fully asleep either. When John stoops to kiss him, his eyes open and there is a terrible, alien wildness in them. A moment later, he flails his arms out defensively, as if he is having a dream of fighting.

Downstairs, Mary sits with a glass of wine, her book closed in her lap. "It was a lovely party," he says. She smiles and stops smiling. He knows what she wanted—for the boys to have had a small, unforgettable adventure, and to have sat politely with their cake, recounting it, thanking her. The measure of her success is thirty years away—will they tell their children about the dragon party? Will they remember the cake shaped like a tower? She has the impulse to plant memories in them, to ensure that their childhoods are happy by stuffing them with discrete, memorable events. The boys were happy, are happy.

"Roger seems to have a fever," he says.

"Yes, I know."

"Probably just worn out from the excitement." As if the force of the day, the intention of filling him with memories has overwhelmed his capacity to receive them. John looks at her with great tenderness, feeling all at once her yearning to be good, to have done well. He wants to embrace her, but she has opened her book.

John retreats upstairs and takes off his tuxedo jacket and his stiff shoes. He looks in again on Oliver and then Roger. His younger son is huddling, asleep, in a small corner of his bed. John climbs in next to him and wraps his son in his arms.

He has read that our instruments can detect energy entering the solar system with the force of a single snowflake striking the ground. He smiles to think of alarmed scientists, red lights flashing and dials oscillating, their scopes trained on this small, radiant nova of warmth. His son's fever seems necessary then, not dangerous or alien; it is his son's body, like his own, healing, learning to heal, to be resilient, being shaped.

Flash of Blue Catches
in a Corner of the Hippocampus
Rebecca Aronson

What the eye sees and does not want it winks inside

ituelʔ uɪ̃cɪypɪ̃ː Lɪː u.ɪ.ɪe·ɪ Tlɪː ɪɪ ɪɪɪɪ ʒ,ɪɪpɪ̃ɪ

    where things slide through: rainy Thursday,
from a bus window a bent bird winging
open into a blue dome above a slickered crowd
and you are eight and lost: a rush of hems and strangers' backs,
jostle of boots, a damp stampede. Your world
    out of reach, neighborhood gone, friends, the low wall
behind the school, all gone in the seconds it took
to drop your hand and step away, look around, find yourself
    nowhere near knowing where you are—then the familiar
gloved grasp, still hurrying on. They would never know
how badly missing you had been.

Coachwhip
JOHN LANE

Padgett's need to be comfortable hits him just before we start walking the final half-mile to the abandoned quarry, so he changes clothes with the pickup's door open between David's sister, Betsy, and Padgett's boxer shorts and bare legs. The blue rain jacket borrowed from me is the first to go, draped over the open passenger door. It's finally stopped raining, and the May sun is out.

When Padgett emerges from behind the dark blue door he is dressed for Southern summer already, in the long khaki shorts he had worn on the flight the day before. He has on a khaki shirt and a wide, brown leather belt cinched up a notch more than seems necessary. I look down and he is also wearing what he calls his "coachwhip catching shoes," a well-worn set of Docksiders with no socks.

Then Padgett takes off down the trail behind Ab, David, and Betsy. His mood seems reflective, even somber. Maybe he is expectant, as a visitor is often expectant in a new landscape. For me, these young Piedmont woods are home base, the furniture of a deep, psychic comfort. Something lined up in me thirty years earlier when I first visited this abandoned quarry. When I stepped out of the truck I felt like I was suddenly rooted as deeply as a white oak. I wrote my first poem, "Collecting Snakes at the Abandoned Granite Quarry," after visiting this quarry. David and I caught a coachwhip on that visit, an elusive snake known for its bad temper. When I first saw the place, I passed like some insect through metamorphosis, from college student to poet, though that student poem did not make me famous, as Padgett's first novel, *Edisto*, had made him.

In the decades that followed there were many more poems for me, but I also began writing essays—long and short—about places like this abandoned quarry. I am interested in speaking for places that have become sanctuary through neglect, abandonment, or abuse. In other words, I became interested in most of the old South—abandoned rice fields, old canals, Piedmont quarries, collapsed mountain house sites deep in recovering woods. What interests me is that I imagine and encounter creatures in these places that don't seem affected by the world closing in around them. There are snakes, lizards, salamanders, frogs, and toads living their lives untroubled—or so it seems on the surface—by the sprawl and spread of urban comfort zones. Even though populations may be endangered, individuals of a particular species are carrying on. It is in these places I have always practiced a "catch and release" sort of amateur herpetology learned in college from true scientists David and Ab, and today I'm returning to it.

At a question-and-answer session the day before, I had asked Padgett why it is that Southern writers so often set their stories in places they've made up, yet his novel *Edisto* will forever be associated with a real place, a sea island down the coast from Charleston.

Padgett fielded my question and considered my notion that a real landscape and his imaginary setting might be confused, that somehow his story could be laid like a grid map or a survey over an actual island. Earlier in the session he had explained how for him the story of precocious Simons Manigault began as "an insupportable notion"—that of a fourteen-year-old writing a novel—and he had taken the notion to its extreme. If the narrative had "collapsed" early, it would have ended up a short story. But as he wrote, the notion extended itself with energy into several hundred pages, and in the end, the notion became *Edisto*, not an island but a novel.

So character and plot and setting are not to be confused with a real place? "Those people on Edisto with my book on their coffee table will be surprised if they ever read it," Padgett said in answer to my inquiry about place. "It's not Edisto. I just wanted to set it between Charleston and Savannah."

Since yesterday I have pondered Padgett's answer with the perplexed aesthetic of a personal essayist. I write about real places and people—like this granite quarry. I don't make much up. I create a solid conceit to work from—that the world exists. In my essay work I try to walk a ridge top trail between imagination and reality. It's different territory than that of a fiction writer like Padgett. The drop-off for me is distinct in either direction—imagination on one side, and fact on the other. I know when I'm off the trail in either direction. The fiction writer walks always in the rich bottomland of the imagination. The trail of fact leads the writer into the imagination's thicket.

~

Still too early in the morning for snake catching, we walk up a very real, rain-soaked trail, once county road, now mealy asphalt softened by corrosive vines and invading grass. "It gives me great hope to see how quickly a road can be dissolved," Ab says, returning to this place after twenty years away.

Padgett listens quietly to Ab's observations and David joking with me. Ab is walking point, his binoculars suspended around his neck. David, in shorts like Padgett, cracks on me, says that he remembers only one snake we ever caught at the old quarry back in college, and so maybe I should go back and rename that first poem, "Collecting Snake at the Abandoned Granite Quarry." I admit to him that memory is a slippery thing, the imagination stretching its constraints and pulling at reality like the roots of poison ivy vines on the road we walk.

It occurs to me that this is how real experience is transformed into art. Fiction would be easier. Change the names, let the place serve the story, make it up. Maybe ten years from now Padgett will find a way to turn this day in South Carolina into a novel, to follow the notion of us all together toward story, but for me the outing is pure nonfiction. It was essay, a true, literary set-up, from the moment I conceived this trip.

I did not coerce Padgett to come snake hunting with us, though I did offer him money for the reading, and he might claim that I as much as promised him a very real coachwhip. If Padgett checked his field guide before boarding the plane to fly north, he might not have been very hopeful. In Spartanburg County, we are at the western limits of the snake's range.

The coachwhip David and I caught in the very quarry we approach had been an adult, about three feet long. I remember the snake had a large dark fierce head, but soon, a foot down its slender explosive body, the color changed to light brown. I don't think it bit either of us when it was caught. I like to think about how the creature actually looks like a coachwhip, the scales on the snake's side were so distinct that they looked like braided leather, and the head looked like a black leather handle. Is it nature's own onomatopoeia?

I know what the snake we caught over a quarter-century ago looked like because I still have a slide that I took in 1976, the snake active and cornered among pine stray and granite rip-rap on the quarry floor. The creature is kinetic, ready to jump out of the small frame. Written in my college scrawl below the image is "Coachwhip, Pacolet, SC." The date stamp by the developer tells me it had been November when we caught the snake, or maybe it was earlier, and I had been lazy getting the film developed. Facts become slippery over time.

As we walk toward the quarry, David narrates what he remembers of catching the coachwhip—how we had seen the snake sunning high on the cliff on a ledge of granite. Ab listens, then adds that he, too, has seen a coachwhip at the quarry years ago, a juvenile. Padgett listens closely to this brief natural history of the quarry. It's not much to work with, but a compelling introduction to this quarry, fraught with serpents.

Padgett's seen several coachwhips in his native Florida. The individuals he's seen fled just like the field guide says they would—"with a burst of speed." His comments suggest he knows their reputation for being savage fighters when cornered, and I think that is one reason he has come north, to test the observation and maybe see one cornered. The possibility of catching the wily coachwhip is like some plot point in a story, a character just off-stage with a loaded gun—in the case of the coachwhip, a nasty set of tiny teeth.

I met Padgett at a gathering of writers in Nashville and we struck up a conversation over dinner not about books, but about snakes and snake hunting. For some reason I thought of the quarry when we began to talk, and at that moment, I imagined bringing him here to this Spartanburg County place, a wild spot I had not seen in over twenty-five years. And soon after, I imagined asking my college friend David, and my friend and former teacher Ab, to come along as well for a snake-catching reunion. We had not been in the field together in twenty years, but I could see the four of us walking with Padgett in the quarry, looking for snakes.

Now we are all here, five people—including David's sister—with different lives drawn together by this swift, elusive creature. As Padgett and I have literature as a mutual field of endeavor, my two old friends David and Ab have backgrounds in the science, reptile and amphibian fieldwork, and wildlife biology. Betsy, David's sister, is a mountain homesteader and bronze caster, and has shown up by chance.

Padgett can't help but notice this is a real place, obviously familiar to his hosts, a place of almost mythic proportions to them. I watch how he reacts. Padgett listens to stories and observations, our old field jabber. He seems intrigued with the place's possibilities. As we walk the road in, he looks at the edges, the ecotones, shifting his eyes as David and Ab do along the margins, looking for movement and shifts in patterns.

For David's sister, Betsy, the quarry floats in deep high school memory only as a possible field trip with a legendary biology teacher. "It could have been some other quarry," she says as we walk in and approach the drop-off. Looking over into the depths she adds, "Now I'm not sure."

Padgett hasn't said much on this outing. Maybe he isn't comfortable among strangers yet. I'm sure he doesn't know exactly what to expect. I haven't figured out much about him since he arrived. We are both writers and should have some things in common, but unlike other literary visitors, he seems bored talking about his books, so I don't ask many literary questions, especially about *Edisto*.

The night before, after his reading at the college and a dinner among colleagues, I had given him a ride back to the hotel. Padgett stood with the truck door open and told me not to get my hopes up about returning to this abandoned quarry after twenty-five years. Then he leaned into the cab and told me a story of how once he had tried to return to an old barrow pit of his childhood in north Florida. It was a place where he had learned to love and fear snakes. He remembered how as a child he had seen indigo snakes "crossing and recrossing the trail into the place." He said he wanted to catch them so bad he had devised a plan of throwing forked sticks at them from a great distance. "You know how when you are scared but you want something so much?"

When he finally went back and looked for the place as an adult all he found was "a new subdivision with bigger houses." Even the barrow pit was gone, and in its place, "was a lake with a little island and paddle boats."

At the abandoned quarry's apex I feel lucky because I see that Padgett is wrong about this place of memory. The quarry site is still just as I remembered it from twenty-five years before. The quarry drops away, not an industrial pit with water in the bottom, but something from an earlier time of industry, a giant V carved out of an accessible hillside, like the Vietnam Memorial with trees and shattered granite on its floor.

I walk to the lip and look down sixty feet. An old stone mason in Spartanburg has told me there are broken columns cut for the state capital in Columbia in the 1860s abandoned among the stunted pines and scattered hardwoods. I hope my morning in the quarry will either prove him right or wrong. Confirming this little scrap of history is something I want maybe as much as Padgett wants a coachwhip.

It is a beauty spot. I gaze from the lip of the quarry out over what must be fifteen miles of Piedmont woods with the quarry sunk like an arrowhead among them. The distance seizes my perspective and grounds it like lightning at the horizon. There is power in layer upon layer of green lingering in the morning light, so rich and new and unpredictable.

Driving in, we passed the working quarry with granite dust and tractors and the gaping hole in the earth. It had been the opposite of this open sky, an engineered hole in the earth inching further outward toward valuable mysteries like this old quarry every afternoon at three when they blast more rock loose from the walls. But on the verge of the old quarry, we could be on another planet except for the occasional warning horns in the distance as the trucks back up to receive their loads of gravel to hump out to the growing county's paving contractors.

On the quarry's perimeter? we walk a huge flat granite outcrop covered with moss and stained dark brown and silver with chemical weathering. We walk down its sloping surface and notice the area sprinkled with the core waste of granite drills. They are two to six inches long and caught in little pockets of moss all down the slope where the sheet wash of storm run-off has left them. They look like little columns or, as Padgett comments, "stone, round Lincoln logs." We pick them up, taking them back as paperweights.

As Padgett walks down the sloping stone he stops, his Docksiders splayed out around a clump of moss, stoops, and picks up a perfect projectile point left suspended on a column of red mud, napped from ruddy chert, the point has been broken off, but there is no mistaking the steady work of human intention and imagination on this chip of stone.

We speculate on how long ago this point has been lost or abandoned. Three hundred years? Three thousand? Padgett pockets the artifact, a fetish for future memory, and we walk on down the slope toward the quarry floor.

I am surprised by the richness of the rubble distributed on this huge flat of stone. My memories of trips here in college do not include this sloping expanse of rock. All I remember is the deep quarry with its dark, fractured walls. I envy Padgett this stone syllable from the story of the quarry's past. Laid side-by-side with the drill corings and the beer cans abandoned on the trail, this point makes a sentence out of human occupation—aboriginal, early American, post-industrial.

The sun is highlighting the south edge of the quarry. We know it's where we should go if we want to find serpents. Ab works on down through stunted sweet gums, cedars, and pines, steps off a solid shelf of granite to the quarry's needle-softened floor where a pine had died and the stump still stands. He strips bark, looking for small snakes or salamanders that might seek shelter in the ruin. David is already walking the long line of industrial moraine that juts out from the short side of the quarry. Within moments of descent to the floor he's spotted a snake. "Black rat snake," he says and moves fast, catching the snake's tail before it disappears among the rubble.

We pass the snake among us. I hold it and sharp musk rises from my hands, a smell common to my youthful snake catching. The rat snake is calm and twists about slowly. I finally pass it to Padgett, who holds it, too, gazing at the black, coiling wildness in his hands. "It's not a coachwhip, but we won't walk away empty-handed," I say.

"Before you go off to the middle of nowhere we better go fishing, to ratify our experience together," Simons Manigault says to his friend and mentor, Taurus, in *Edisto*. The two characters are fishing for mullet in a chapter. The day before Padgett had told an audience at Wofford that it's the only one in the novel where, "everything is true." He explained to the afternoon session how this scene happened and he just wrote it down, inserting Simons and Taurus in replacement for himself and a friend. Maybe fishing, the act of securing from the world its riches, is beyond fiction. As Simons says, it ratifies.

They fished, and we hunt. Holding this first snake has ratified my experience with Padgett, not the reading the night before. Not the talk of books and publishing. Here is something unpracticed and raw for two writers to exchange, something moving between us that does not need an agent. David has caught this place's long muscular center for us, and passed it along to admire and then release back into the world. Maybe that's what's strange about art. A novel or story composed and abandoned by its author never settles back into the experiential world from which it came. It remains a human artifact, like this quarry, a space utilized, a beautiful human scar upon the landscape. An essay serves a little different purpose. Often the world stays with it. They say a fact is that which can be confirmed, and personal essays are often full to the brim with facts.

At the reading the night before, *Edisto* had not been on Padgett's play list as I had secretly hoped it would be. He had searched at the podium instead among a loose sheaf of fresh pages, stories published and unpublished what he called "a failed novel" about Boris Yeltsin, two short, dream-like tales titled "South Carolina" and "Florida." The work seemed wild and elusive. The audience laughed. He commented on how uncertain he was about what he would read next. He wandered among this raw material of fiction like a man looking for a trail into the deeper woods. After an hour, at 8:30, he stopped abruptly, thanked us for our attendance. "That was a strange little reading," Padgett said, stepping out from behind the podium.

What do we know of a place? Does it come from the keen eye of a naturalist, or the stories we carry away? Between the five of us there are as many answers. For another hour we explore the ridge of rubble, and Ab points out fence lizards abundant among the slabs and deadfall and speaks their scientific name, *sceloporus*, and places the creature within a web of his deep knowing.

Walking the high, dark north wall of the quarry I spot one more snake on a bench of granite. "The mother of all hognoses," Ab calls it as we approach. Everyone walks over and admires the three-foot relaxed eastern hognose with the distinct, turned-up snout. Padgett picks it up and holds this snake, then puts it down, this triggering its defensive stance, the cobra-like spreading of neck that prompted the nonpoisonous hognose's common name, "spreading adder." Ab picks it up and explains how rarely they bite, but how painful it can be if they do. There's a long tooth in the snake's throat "used to deflate toads," its primary food source.

As we leave the hognose where we found it, I comment with audible regret to Padgett that we've not seen the coachwhip, or found the columns of the old capital. He puts the hognose back on its altar of granite, says he thinks that what we have experienced is actually better. We've found two snakes we could hold calmly in our hands. Padgett's right. The coachwhip remains more powerful as a hidden mystery, and the abandoned capital columns as a story the stonemason believes and will continue to pass along.

Edisto is still in print, even if Padgett doesn't read from it these days. Simons Manigault now sleeps between the covers of a book almost twenty-years-old. Each time someone buys it, teaches it, or checks it out of the library, it's as if this bright sun has hit a sloping face of granite.

A good story is as real and elusive as a coachwhip. The world lights up not suddenly from above, but with brightness leaking out of a familiar landscape, from cracks and fissures in the stone. I walk on, intent on this return to the place of my youthful poetizing. Not even the trucks hauling the rock away in the distance can bring me out of the light's sudden revelry, and the rediscovered wilderness of my own perception.

The Ecotone Interview

Rick Bass is the author of more than twenty books of fiction and nonfiction, including *Where the Sea Used to Be, Colter: The True Story of the Best Dog I Ever Had*, and, most recently, *The Diezmo*. In 2002, he edited *The Roadless Yaak: Reflections and Observations About One of Our Last Great Wilderness Areas*, a collection of essays about Yaak Valley by writers, philosophers, scientists, loggers, and hunters. Bass' short stories have been anthologized in the *Best American Short Stories* and *O. Henry Award* series. He lives with his family and works in Yaak Valley, Montana, where he is a member of the Yaak Valley Forest Council, the Montana Wilderness Association, the Round River Conservation Studies, and the Cabinet Resource Group. Bass was the Writer-in-Residence in the MFA program at UNCW during the spring of 2005.

with Rick Bass
KIMI FAXON

KIMI FAXON: You've said that writing cannot be taught, but that the habits of a writer can be. How has this played out for you? I am wondering how you became a writer, how you learned your habits, and which writers you would cite as major influences.

RICK BASS: It continues to play out every day. Particularly with my desires to spend time with family, and with the ever-expanding tasks of activism during a neoconservative government, it's more important than ever to try to carve out, and keep carved out, a couple of hours a day in which to be a writer and to remember how to be a writer, which in large part is to say, to remember how not to be anything else, so that you can inhabit your story that day as if for the first time. To bring freshness to it.

I became a writer largely by and after reading Jim Harrison's title novella, *Legends of the Fall*. Harrison, Tom McGuane, and numerous other western writers were early influences, as much for their lifestyles— spending time out of doors and managing to make a living without having to teach. That was, and is, appealing to me. Teaching is wonderful, and an absolutely honorable profession, but in addition to sucking away from one's own work, it also can pull one away from the business of living. It is an enormous obligation, particularly when done properly.

FAXON: You once said that you "look for the world" as a fiction writer, and that for you there is little difference between fiction and nonfiction. Can you speak about the way you look for and to the world for story, and how you make the decision to shape that narrative into fiction or nonfiction, or, in other words, how and why you employ each genre?

BASS: Part of it probably has to do with how hungry I am to write a short story, but I do believe also that certain immeasurable ideas, elements, voices, structures, do combine with the writer's temperament at any given time to predispose a story toward fiction, rather than nonfiction. For lack of a better word, there is a kind of electricity or vitality that attends the beginnings of fiction for me, an otherworldliness and inexplicable-ness, whereas the condition preceding the beginning of a piece of nonfiction is generally calmer, less electrical, less wondering, less-less.

FAXON: Many consider you to be a member of the canon of nature writers in America, but much of that writing about nature and place has come out of your fiction. Some say that nature writing has been boxed off as a genre, relocated to its own section in bookstores. You are a writer who seems to have broken out of that box. Can you discuss this? Do you feel that fiction has been the best means for you to write about place?

BASS: The increase in place-based literature in the nonfiction genre has certainly been prolific, often in the celebratory mode (other times in lamentation)—I wonder if affording place the import of a character in a fiction story might not sometimes be a higher accolade to that place.

As far as box-breaking, it may be as much a function of subject and genre diversity that sometimes allows me a little breathing room in the Nature Writer thing. While there are nature writers out there, and certainly it's a wonderful thing to be, there are also an awful lot of writers out there who are being called Nature Writers who are actually just plain old writers. In the end it doesn't matter—if the writer writes well enough, and movingly enough, then the readers will be moved, changed, and such notions of categorization won't trouble their mind. The point that the subject, the classification, is being discussed can sometimes be a tip-off that something in the text might benefit from some work.

FAXON: The theme of this issue is migration and movement. While there is a great Thoreauvian tradition of American writers who write out of their commitment to home, there is also the opposite tradition of those who write in exile; Hemingway in Paris comes to mind. You are very much a "home" writer, but also someone who travels widely for your work; how has this affected you and your writing? Do you think is it necessary for a writer to claim a place as home?

Bass: It's absolutely not necessary for a writer to claim a place as home—I think imagination is the one tool most critical to a writer. For me, place, and an understanding of a place's logic and systems, expands imagination. So it's useful—and attractive—to me, for that. For me, place, and the processes of place—particularly undeveloped nature—is the genesis, the bedrock, of imagination.

Faxon: I once heard John Elder say that we call a place wilderness when it does not contain our stories. You write in the last paragraph of the essay "River People" from *Wild to the Heart*, "If it's wild to your own heart, protect it. Preserve it. Love it. And fight for it, and dedicate yourself to it, whether it's a mountain range, your wife, your husband, or even (heaven forbid) your job. It doesn't matter if it's wild to anyone else: if it's what makes your heart sing, if it's what makes your days soar like a hawk in the summertime, then focus on it. Because for sure, it's wild, and if it's wild, it'll mean you're still free. No matter where you are." What do think distinguishes wilderness from wildness, and can we live in the midst of both anymore?

Bass: I use the phrase "wilderness" almost as a legal term, usually to refer to big tracts of undeveloped country, often though not always possessing great or significant biological diversity, and often possessing its own highly developed system of logic and natural processes, while "wildness" is perhaps a simpler abstraction, referring simply to that which skitters away from human control.

Faxon: For much of the last decade, you have used your writing to support your activism. Do you think of your writing and your activism as complementary? What happens when you come to writing with an intention, a call to arms, an awareness, instead of a poetic impulse that I've heard you talk about? Others have warned of this, the tendency to marry one's art to one's politics. Are there dangers to this? What is gained? What is lost, if anything?

Bass: This is a hard question to answer. I hate answers that are ambiguous, the sometimes-yes and sometimes-no variety, but that's the case here. Perhaps the foremost danger in bringing intent to your writing lies in the fact that the imagination can be quickly compromised—

choices can seem too obvious, lines too direct. Revelation can substitute for discovery. The rapport between writer and reader is all-important, and when you're using the reader for your own political perspective, well, that's a tricky game even on its own face, but even more so if your goal is to produce something artistic. The further into this I get as a writer, with so little tangible gain (none, yet, in the Yaak) having come from so many tens of thousands of pages, the more I wonder if the only real gains are of a personal nature—the repeated call to arms, stepping up to speak out against injustice, the unwillingness to accept such.

The losses, of course, come in the realm of art—the plaguing notions of what could have been written, what could have been imagined, otherwise, were one not engaged in the war of one's activism. But I would not want to be the kind of person who loved the Yaak landscape as much as I do, and found it as special as I do, who then turned his back on speaking out for its protection.

Tourist Canoe
ANDREW GOTTLIEB

Always like this: the thunk of paddle on gunwale.
Lifted wood turns pond drip to ripples,
and the glide of the curved bow spears the surface
in a silent vee your pressed blade makes.
This is you alone, your body levering the boat
ahead, hull rolling with your tensed weight,
your hips pleased with the lean and lull of the shell
on clear water, the slow shift of the far-off shore.
In the bow, a bag of rock for balance. The surface
resists your sink with its flared palm, your float:
this delicate measure of spread and pressure.
Below your stroke, boulders sit deep in the green
murk, glacial remains dragged and dropped
with an age that makes you afraid. This is you
alone, skimming along the surface again
with the flexed effort your body allows, mere feet
from the cold underneath the lake freely shows.
This is you seeing the dark fish float
over the rock you fear, the salmon's black back
still for a moment in the cold lake, the slack body,
hovering mid-water below your boat
before a gill-flare and a rippling fin tip you off
to the flicker of a swift single surge. You stare.
There's just a rock, and this is you, adrift
with your lean and your look, your shadow,
the paddle, your stiff imitation.

Eight Paintings
BARBARA FISHER

"Places in-between" have always fascinated me and informed my work. Not being familiar with the word "ecotone" before the birth of this journal, I nevertheless feel as if I have been living in one for as long as I can remember. As has my artwork.

To paraphrase the definition given in the first volume, "eco" = dwelling and "tone" = tension. Houses are one of many familiar iconic forms in my work. They have always represented The Self to me, and as such are placed in mysterious situations, with varying degrees of stability/instability. They sit on the edge, attempting to find balance in an unfamiliar landscape. Glowing rocks/eggs also sit precariously, and strange, long-legged creatures often appear. Simple botanical forms grow from all directions.

The "meaning" of each piece is open to interpretation: Is this a gravity-free zone? Are the creatures friendly or menacing? Could the abyss into which the vases or houses or chairs are falling be a better world? Are these figures and plants and rocks communicating across the borders that seem to separate or strand them? Are they trying to get out or stay safe? I'm not sure. I just paint what I see.

Beneath the Surface

My Soul to Take

Night Vision

Before I Wake

A Home Away From Home II

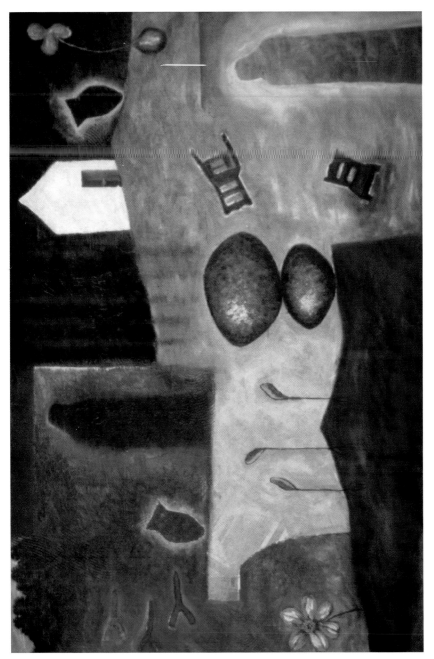

Silent Conversation

Precarious Promise

Holding the World Together

Béti Leaves: Cultural and Political Borders
Margo Tamez

That fence is a political border—
not a cultural one.
                    —José Emiliano Garcia

I unload her laundry, and stack it neatly to the side, where she'll pick it up to hang on the line. It is late August, and the sky contains scarce moisture in its evaporating horsetail clouds. Flirtatiously, the monsoon arrives on cool breezes that come from the mountain updrafts and the Sea of Cortez. They lure me to the north side of the trailer. I aim to get chores over with by mid-morning, to be inside and do absolutely nothing but sit on a chair that won't stick to my thighs and leave behind two shining ovals on the wooden seat. The twins of those wet flat eyes on the backs of my thighs, the soft, nearly invisible hair there doing what evolution meant for it to do—provide a way to cool my limbs, the silken hairs providing an evaporative cooling apparatus that triggers upon contact with air and instantly sets off a mini ventilating scheme in each pore. One of the beautiful little miracles of the architecture called the human body.

I'll take off my shirt when everyone else is outside working in the gardens thirsty for water, though they get a deep soak every other day and thrive under thick mulch and complimentary legumes and plentiful canopy of mesquites. We encourage the volunteer mesquites wherever we can, a way to reclaim the once healthy and herbaceous northern Sonoran ecosystem on a three-acre demonstration farm, yet the salinity and nitrates from years of chemicals, contributed by previous farmers from the post-war era through the present, challenge our most skilled organic and biodynamic methods to reclaim the soil—and the soul—of this land.

I put my gloves down on the floor next to my chair; my neck and head rest on the bony back of the thriftstore Shaker replica, with a few more months left in its rickety frame. Not a plush recliner of my fantasies, but it will do as I close my eyes by the nearest swamp cooler vent, languishing in its promise of mental transport to a cooler clime, say . . . Glacier National Park, or Anchorage . . . I'm not picky. Just one or two breath-filled moments before the kids burst through the door wanting lunch.

Today is my turn to wash laundry. I have a cooperative arrangement with the Mexican migrant workers who rent living space from me in a traditional O'odham earth and frame house, called a "sandwich" house that they helped my family build this past spring. A humble and ingenious living shelter utilizing the raw materials of the desert—abundant clay and sand-filled soil, saguaro ribs or old two-by-fours as substitutes, dried ocotillo branches, water, shovels, strong arms and willing backs—the sandwich house of the O'odham people reveals their long and intimate relationship with the Sonoran desert ecosystem and the oral tradition emergent from this symbiotic affiliation which informs their 'himdak,' or 'way of life,' a life inherently in tune with cycles of the desert, and one engaged in a profound struggle against inclusion on the endangered list.

I fondly recall that day spent raising walls and eating a barbecued pig the men slaughtered. While they carefully peeled the skin off the animal, and sliced it into small wedges for deep frying chicharrones, a delicacy they crave, known as pork rinds to non-Indian and non-Spanish speaking cultures. I helped butcher the pig to freezable parts, passed around cheap, cold beer from the local farmers' convenience store (the only store within fourteen square miles), and made pico de gallo for the pork tacos we'd be savoring way past the sunset of a brewing monsoon.

The migrants and I use the washing machine on alternate days. We use a second-hand machine, bought at another thriftstore in Casa Grande which is owned by a Mexican-American family who repair a variety of household machines ready for resale to a largely labor and blue-collar community in a mostly rural county. Most folks I've encountered during the nine years I've resided in Pinal county do not have full-time employment, and as a matter of pride consider buying anything new an embarrassing, if not downright shameful expenditure of hard-earned and hard-gotten 'frog skins,' 'mula,' 'bolas,' —*cash*.

~

We wash our laundry either early in the morning, or after sundown to preserve the rebuilt machine's stamina and to conserve precious water. Without a roof above to protect its hard-working motor from the kiln of monsoon season, the sun fatigues its ability to wash too many loads from July through September, with temperatures notoriously peaking between 115 and 120 degrees. At a sustainable house demonstration in Tucson, I witnessed a community that did all their wash with a motor hooked up by a belt to a two-wheeled bicycle, run by the residents. All their community members had attractive, muscular calves.

Today I have heaps of sheets from the kids' beds, and as I unload Béti's wash, a swift regret creeps upon me. Taking out her load of clothes, I imagine a map of her personal to do list, which preoccupies me. I put her things in a neat pile on the table we use next to the machine for organizing our laundry activities, and I follow the flyway: two pair of athletic shoes, a bra, two jersey T-shirts, a pair of black hip-hugger shorts, a green canvas travel bag, and a stuffed rag doll that she washes every so often like a ritual remedy for comfort and longing.

There is a familiar connection of one of her personal belongings to one strand of my consciousness, or déjà vu, or the mere hint of a scent I know from before and all this suddenly rushes me, lifting small hairs on my arms. I see what's coming next.

She's leaving. Within one day. I know this feeling and don't question it. This sudden shift in sense and perception—quivering locust, to mountain lion, to hummingbird. She holds these changes in common with the twist of wind that all the migrants who I've sheltered over nine years share—immediate adaptation, transparency, swift transformation, flight.

The commons she shares with her countrywomen are not the presumed commons many of us presume and conceptualize as our natural rights—air, water, land, a healthy planet. The legacy she endures includes the dispassionate, the impersonal, and the often dangerous conditions of survival. Her choices are narrow. If she didn't locate me by word of mouth, her alternative consisted of the barracks, where money-grabbing coyotes and clusters of men with no family or contacts prey on naïve and gullible victims. Many migrants get used for their precious and hard-earned cash to pay for gasoline on dead-end journeys to Texas, Florida, and other places hungry for servitude guised as employment. Others will stumble into the paths of the *migra*—the border patrol, who scour State Route 347 or Highway 84 searching for illegals, only to return them to the border where other dimensions and layers of poverty, displacement, and oppression await them.

In the barracks, laborers endure employers who frequently neglect paying them when obligated, and who may eventually be the anonymous caller to alert the *migra* at the end of a season in order to avoid paying the last paycheck of a brutally hot and desperate season. And they're all desperate. Here in the rural desert, perhaps only turkey buzzards persistently harvesting carrion are the ones carrying forward the enduring stories of us, witnessing the human folly high above ground.

Ritualistic consumption. Cyclical denial. Dodging accountability. The embarrassingly over-privileged and the masses of poor.

Our conversation of the other day comes rushing forward. Mentally preparing to make her journey back to her home community in Mexico, a couple of hundred miles down Mexico's Pacific Coast, to deliver six months of wages to her mother, reunite with her children for a week, and then make the journey back to the border for a ride to Florida with a coyote and a truck full of workers, she reasoned with me in Spanish to not be pessimistic as we prepared the masa for tortillas out under the shade of the ramada.

"With little work for the women here in the field, why should I stay?" she explained, adjusting her sunglasses and pulling the rim of her wide straw hat lower to keep the sun from irritating her eyes.

"Being here with the babies, your children, makes me ache in my heart every night for my own little ones."

She paused, turning her head to watch my kids take turns on the old slide salvaged from the landfill on the local Indian reservation. Lovingly, she scolds the older two for not allowing the toddler to scale the ladder first. Then she turned back to me, not wanting me to notice how her chin quivered. She struggled. I touch her shoulder softly, not wanting to embarrass her, but wanting her to know I hear.

"My mother can't go it alone ..." she continued." She wants her life back, you know, it's expensive to feed them all, which leaves nothing for her if she wants something for herself, like going to the doctor, or getting medicine."

Her eyes caught mine, and then quickly looked away. For an instant I saw resentment toward her mother, and simultaneous guilt, frustration, and worry.

I wanted to say something to encourage her, though I knew she didn't want encouragement, she had made up her mind. She wanted me to let go. She wanted me to offer her a job. She wanted me to help her bring her kids up here. She wanted to be me, the one *she* saw—American, a landowner, educated, with means to grab hold and shape life into what I wanted.

No matter how severe my personal struggles, the fact that my privileges enable me to access resources beyond her grasp, by way of class, education, and nationality, exposed the chasm between us. No matter how much I tried to bridge that expanse it pushed hard against me. It was then I finally recognized the castes she and I imagined and lived daily. My own experience of caste in America I hold closely and curse in my deepest despair and fervent struggles against systems laden with corruption. Her knowledge and easy acceptance of the caste she implicitly recognized, which swelled and tossed like a dark sea between us, stilled me. We finished our work in silence.

Washing our faces and hands before making supper is a daily ritual to wash off residues of pesticides and herbicides sprayed every night and morning in our area because of the cotton-growing season. Pesticides, which the farmers don't have to divulge to the public, despite state laws which try to enforce compliance, seep into our bloodstream through our skin, mouth and nasal membranes. No matter how many times a person calls the Department of Environmental Quality, which oversees rural areas, the politics of agriculture in this county outweigh the risks to human health. We made white foamy suds up and down our arms and hands until they were red.

While we washed she hinted at her plan. Saying the plan out loud—as if saying and hearing it helped her firm up the decision, like a clay body she alone had to shape, carve, polish, and fire. She defined her limits and permitted me to know how easily she could fail. Yet, there is no room for failure. I'm reminded of my mother. I'm reminded of myself. This is so natural, this acceptance of extreme risk, cause, and effect. The familiar rational edifice that Mexican-Indian women slip over their skin as easy as embroidered *rebozos* reconfiguring our poverty, beautifying it, making it bearable. I've learned this gesture implicitly from my mother—and find I often practice it involuntarily. Living with Béti, confronting these disparities forces me to unlearn it.

Shaking her head side to side, she continued, "Only men are needed in the chile fields; the notice was given to all the women at the lunch break today . . . so . . . maybe I'll try my luck in Florida, when I return."

"Return?" I answered, quickly, not really surprised, passing her a saltén, frying pan, to refry the frijoles we made on Sunday.

"Oh yes. I have to see what the problem is with my mother. Then when all is settled, I will come back." She spoke again about going to Florida with a group of men from Sonora who were going that way. I cautioned her about traveling such a long distance. The danger of crossing the Sonoran desert, and the horror stories of going through Texas. The lower Rio Grande valley is some of the most treacherous territory since the implementation of NAFTA. Fear gripped me. Did she know these men? How would she get back to Sonora if she got picked up by the *migra* in Texas, or Florida? Did she have any security that there'd really be work for her in Florida? Or would the coyotes rob her of her meager savings just to get themselves there, and dump her? We'd both heard of women being brutally assaulted en route across the long and difficult trek throughout the Southeast region. That would put her thousands of miles further from her community of Caborca.

She lowered her eyes, acknowledging and confirming that she had the same concerns.

Her clothes are few, neat, easily carried in her canvas bag. A part of me wants her to stay, though I cannot offer her the income she must make to support her children in Caborca; and I feel guilty having another woman doing my own housecleaning and cooking, even though I am recovering from a difficult birth. I think her experience in *el norte* is bitterly disappointing. Mexican-Indian nationals are one of the lowest castes here in southern Arizona, lower than non-B.I.A., non-enrolled Mexican-Americans, who are the lowest Indians on the North American totem pole.

I touch her small pile of belongings. She and I are friends, if only for a few months. We give aid to each other and know this affinity lasts only briefly. We learn not to think into the future. The clear separation of class she feels towards me is uncomfortable, yet I understand its shape as my own hand; in my own homeland I feel that I am the lowest caste—female, Mexican, Indian. I am caught in my discomfort and don't know how to navigate this psychological space she builds so swiftly between us. Yet her need to construct a buffer between her reality and mine is familiar to me. I've done it all my life under similar circumstances when I am the other. Still, I find it difficult to get used to the sudden absence of the people who share unselfishly with me and teach me so profoundly, careful not to ask for too much.

I feel the absence coming, its inevitability. I grieve the loss of her companionship.

Béti reverently refers to me as La Dona, but I do not see myself as the "dona" she imagines and sees. Yet she forces me to confront my privilege. She shapes me as the other, as different. Much the same way I shape some of my mentors as more economically advantaged and therefore not on the same page.

Béti establishes another border that I don't want between me and another woman of color. It is devastating. She has helped me nurse a newborn child by feeding me and providing me sustenance to create mother's milk; she has made numerous traditional meals of corn masa and fresh garden vegetables to nourish my depressed body and spirit; she has sung songs of old conflicts and women warriors who won and lost; she has been a hearth that I warm my heart to on lonely nights when I wonder, and sometimes doubt, my own purpose and fate.

I feel guilty, and angry, that I can't create an economic opportunity for her in my home, as she had hoped. From her perspective I am a wealthy woman. I own my own land. On a global scale, and even on an American one, that in itself is a rarity. For Béti, like so many, land is our mother. To be able to tend to her, to stand on her barefooted and take responsibility for her as a steward, if only for your lifetime, is still a desirable goal.

Defending earth is the same as defending people, and enlarging the scope of protection to include people in the places where they live, where they work, and where their children play is her fundamental goal which can only be achieved when she is economically stable. Yet, her continued economic instability like that of her her mother and millions like her on both sides of the border, unable to unshackle a status of servitude, often factors strongly in feelings of desperation, depression, and hopelessness. People who are struggling to survive every minute of the day do not often have the capacity to see or believe in the long goals of well-meaning conservation and development aspirations.

The social and human benefits of economic and environmental policies to transform women and children's lives globally is not happening quickly enough for Béti. When I'm called on to participate in retreats with policymakers, officials from NGO's, academics, scientists, farmers, attorneys, funders, and activists on the environment and social justice (often in secluded, pristine locations), Béti is the one on my mind. At one gathering I lost my patience completely with simulations and role-playing exercises facilitated by diversity mediators, and I literally grieved publically in utter frustration and pain because simulations don't translate well when I'm asked to tell a story of my experience. I learned quickly that I had to be cautious about any so-called 'movement' that didn't spend a substantial amount of time focusing on building the bonds between our lives and the common threads of passion, beliefs, dreams, and visions.

A movement that honors my need to share the fragile, delicate story of Béti, because by sharing it I forced myself to face disturbing truths that profoundly altered my personal vision of the world I want to live in. By sharing it I take on a stewardship role of the precious intimacies of the lives revealed and represented by these words on this page. By sharing it I make commitments to honor Béti and all women who the world abuses and neglects. I am profoundly humbled by her realness, and the deficit of tangible changes she experiences because of her gender, race, language, education, age, and nationality. There is no facilitated simulation that comes anywhere near to her small bundle of clothing in my hands as I fold them for her, knowing I may not ever see her again beyond tomorrow, and my desperate will to change these facts.

On the day after I gave birth to my youngest, Béti made me *sopas de arroz* and tortillas. Both my life and my child's had been seriously threatened during the pregnancy. Béti fed me when I had no strength left, when my mother's milk refused to arrive, when I was brokenhearted, when I despaired and made some plans in my journal for my other children in case I died.

When I had no strength to move day after day, she sang to me and urged me on, chasing my blues away with her broom, she'd say. When I regained my strength months later, I felt good when I chased away one of her drunken, jealous lovers who, in a rage, slashed the tires on her car to prove his point. He returned in the middle of the night with his serenading songs of guilt. She laughed and approved when I confronted him and reciprocated his rage with a firm demand to compensate her for her tires and to stay the hell away. Her laughs and gratitude warmed me so.

Her few belongings I respect for their economy. I walk away from them, knowing she'll come for them in the middle of the night. Her ride will come when I'm asleep, and last-minute conversations with me will not deter her from her decision. The midnight coyote will take her across the desert, south to Caborca, a place where desert meets the sea. She will cross *el border*, like a secret, a shadow of knowledge burned off to salmon-pink light in the glare of a turbulent monsoon.

The Mexicali Blues
BRIAN LAIRD

Heart, have no fright.
There on the battlefield
I cannot wait to die
By the blade of sharp obsidian.
Our hearts want nothing but a war death.
                                        —Aztec Poem

*A*rm yourself! Grab a gun, a knife, a rock. Pick up a gnarled old stick of
thick wood and pound a nail through the knotty head.

The handcuffs, slipped loosely around your skinny wrists in the night, are
tightening, tightening.

Wake up, Damn it! I'm the giggling psycho pinching your toe in the pale
light of dawn. You rub your eyes, thinking, What? Am I really here?

Wake up! If you sleep while it gathers its tanks and lines them in the
square, then, too late: tan and relaxed—and handcuffed—you'll stand before
them, blinking. And you'll be crushed. Then forgotten.

Arm yourself. Attack!

THE BURNING EARTH

The ground is darker now. Smoke slips up in places, chemicalearth
combusting spontaneously under the summer sun.

The dirt is actually smoldering here. It is saturated with toxic waste,
and I wonder what would happen if I set a match to it. I pat my pocket,
but find only plastic film canisters—supplies for the day's work.

Steph skids down the embankment to the river's edge. But it is not
a river. Not anymore. The smell overpowers. We have handkerchiefs
knotted behind our necks, covering our mouths and noses, like train
robbers in an old western.

The dirt on the banks is a broken dark brown, like coffee grounds.
But there are veins of white running through it. And the smoke. The
smoke shouldn't be here. The earth shouldn't burn.

She leans close to the water. Not water. Pollution. Toxic waste.

Words aren't strong enough. They can't carry the smell—the chemical stink seeping into your nose and throat, searing your tissues.

She focuses her camera, sets an aperture, and shoots—a thin plant growing in the poison.

She is very near the edge, her feet planted precariously in the soft earth. I think to say, be careful. But I let it go.

Further along I see the legs of an animal sticking out of the paleyellow tall grass on the opposite bank, separated from me by the crawling olive green liquid.

Planks, placed end to end and balanced on car tires, form a precarious bridge that touches the white foam frothing at the riverside. I step onto the cracked wood carefully, knowing that if a board gives or if I move wrong I will fall into the river.

I consider backing out, walking downriver a mile or so, to the bridge where the road crosses. Then I think, the hell with it, and I slip into the dream world:

The wood creaks under my feet. The murky green water seeps up onto the boards, touches the soles of my boots. I can see right where the line breaks, the dryness starts. I feel I can make a slight adjustment and move the line of wetness an exact millimeter higher or lower

Another step and the board moves. I shift my balance, hoping vaguely that the plank will hold. It does, and I step gently off the plank onto the other bank.

It is a calf carcass. Small chickens peck at the skin around its neck and stomach, breaking through tough hide to get at the maggots crawling in the soft flesh. Where the chickens have been pecking, the fur looks like the tussled hair of a child fresh from the tub—blond, matted, and wet.

Up the bank is a shackhouse. A couple of skinny cows, a swayback horse, and these chickens. The chickens eat at the carcass, drink from the polluted stream, and the humans eat the chickens. A natural cycle gone bad. And the people—especially the children—are sick so often that some of them have forgotten they were ever healthy. Just accept it. Part of the routine. Part of the wheel.

They live here because the few remaining factories are here. The *maquilas*. There is work here. Sometimes.

The sun beats down on their rough huts. The factories pollute, the workers pollute. One million people squat together on this flat, hostile piece of desert, where even plants have sense enough to grow far apart.

I shift around but I can't get it all in the frame. My foot slips and I scramble back up the bank. The chickens disappear into the tall grass. I wait, but they don't come back.

I settle for just the calf, with the river beyond. The grass spreads naturally at its hooves, guiding my lens, framing the image. I adjust, shoot. Sweat drips into my right eye as I release the shutter. I ignore it, holding still until blackness clicks the scene from view and the frame is exposed, the deed done.

I rub the sweat away with my shirt sleeve.

I think, that wasn't it. That was not the one. I missed it by just a moment, a fragment. One misstep. The picture I am looking for is still out there, somewhere, unseen.

The hot breeze shifts on the river. Chemicalstink washes through my handkerchief, into my nose and throat. I cough. It feels like ammonia in my lungs, I gasp for air, turn away.

Steph wanders past on the far bank. She doesn't notice the calf. I cross over and catch up with her. We trudge along the river's edge, feet slipping in that soft, chemical earth.

I stop to talk to the owner of one of the shacks. He is short, with a thin, weathered face. He wears a T-shirt, cutoff shorts, straw hat.

I ask if he has noticed the dead calf.

He says no. But he isn't surprised, it is not the first time. And up river, he says, there are other things. Worse things. It is not safe to go there.

I ask if anyone touches the water, drinks it.

No, only a crazy man would.

But the animals.

Yes, the animals. Sometimes they drink there.

He says that he and his wife and children are sick often. But what can he do?

He asks the question hopefully. I have no answer.

He asks what I am doing here, with my camera and my questions.

I try to explain it to him.

He squints, cocks his head to one side. Will you tell them what it is like here, he asks, will you show them how it is?

I will tell them, I say. But they will not listen.

Later, I lean back on my haunches by the crawling green waste.

The sun is high now—nearing three o'clock—and the day is reaching its hottest, somewhere around a 115 degrees.

64

I take off my hat, pull down my bandanna, and sit in the soft dirt. Wipe the sweat from my forehead. Close my eyes.

She snaps open a new film cylinder next to my ear. She is to my right and back a little, laying the film flat in the camera now, and snapping it closed. Her legs are splayed, pushing gentle depressions into the dirt, which reaches greedily to meet them.

She smiles at me and I return her salute. Neither of us really knows what drives. The devil, I've heard. She would probably agree, and we smile that sloppy grin at each other, knowing we share this much: We both have to move, have to go. We cannot sit still.

We help each other up. Move along. Stomping further into Mexico along the soft toxic banks of the river.

THE GAUZE SHROUD

The old man sits under the ratty awning, squinting out at the shattered reality around him. This is his home. No matter that it is also the municipal garbage dump. He has carved out a place for himself here. Home.

His name is Juan. He is missing both arms. Lost in an accident, he says, and no more about it.

He is forty-seven but looks much older to me. For twenty-three years he has lived here on the river's edge. His face is thin, white whiskers stubbled over a sharp chin. The lines worried into his face all cut downward.

Across from us, a tractor rumbles through the trash, pushing mountains of waste toward the river's edge.

I squat down, peering into the shade that surrounds the old man while the sun grinds away at my shoulders, my back.

It has always been a dump, Juan says, but not so bad. It is getting closer and closer, but he doesn't really mind. Much of his home—this shack of cardboard, tin, bailing wire, plastic sheets, without running water, electricity, gas—much of it was salvaged here.

He leans back, tracing a tight circle in the dirt with the big toe of one bare foot.

Four children play in the yard. Dirty, loud—boisterous, even in the heat. They are Juan's grandchildren. He speaks proudly of the nine children he fathered—all of them healthy, he says. Every one. Only one still lives in Mexicali, the mother of these four. The others have scattered into Sonora, Chihuahua, Sinaloa.

I ask about the tractors—the big cats scratching through the litter. I had heard that the Mexican government, under pressure from environmental groups, had closed all the dumps along the New River.

Maybe so, he says, he is not sure.

I hear a strange noise. It comes again—a moan from the shade behind him. For the first time I notice the woman.

She is a gauze bundle stretched on a makeshift cot. Flies buzz around her face and arms. Her breath is a ragged whisper. She shifts to one side and moans again. The movement, apparently, is painful.

Juan calls to the oldest boy, tells him to brush the flies away from his grandmother.

She is very sick, he says, but she will get better. There is no hope in his voice.

The boy tugs the gauze up over her face.

It is in her intestines, he says. It hurts her very much. A friend took her to *Cruz Roja* last week. But the doctor said he did not know what was wrong with her. It is not a bacteria. It is a mysterious new disease. Something they have not seen before. They have no medicine. But she will get better, he says, she will get better.

I begin shooting: the old man, his strained eyes squinting straight ahead, stained shirt with empty sleeves, pants torn at the knee, toes in the dirt. I shift left and the old woman comes into view in the background, the thin gauze covering her face. I breathe out slowly, steadying the lump of metal, circuitry, and ground glass in my hands. And I shoot. I repeat the process many times, changing the settings slightly to make sure one image comes out just right. She is in the deep shade, he in the harsh light—the precise setting of aperture and shutter speed is beyond calculation here in the dust and dirt, when the moment counts and time won't allow for a complicated formula. It is better to shoot all the possibilities. One of them may come out right. One will be right.

When I'm done I thank him for his time.

Where will you go? he asks.

Farther on, I say.

It is too late, he says. It will be dark soon. That direction, the river is no good. There are things happening there that no one should see.

We have to go, I say.

He shakes his head and wishes us luck. As we walk away, the old man sings. His voice is soft and scratchy. I recognize the tune. He is singing the Mexicali blues.

We skirt the tractor—its driver faceless behind a surgeon's mask, does not look at us—and we drop down the bank, following the river.

Farther on, we reach the factories. They spew chemicals into the river. A drain for toxic waste. No surprise. I think of our leader, poster boy for corporate greed. I make plans. We will bring him here, anoint him, baptize him in the waters of industry. His waters. Our waters.

THE GLOW

The factories leave us empty, drained, drenched in sweat and foul chemical odor. They were built hard against the river's edge, and have high, flat, windowless walls, like fortresses in a Kurosawa movie. At the bottom of the walls, drainage pipes empty over the bank. The colors are a dark rainbow: green-yellow, a sick dark brown, and black. Some billow forth hundreds of gallons per minute. Others just trickle.

The chemicalstink coats my skin, my lungs. I feel sick, weak. But we press on, pausing only to take photos—documentary thieves stealing the truth from this dungeon.

Beyond the factories, the river is smaller, the flow weaker. The banks are high and steep, and from the riverside the liquid appears thicker. It has turned white.

Things float by down there. Large things.

We pass a monstrous cattle yard—the shuffling, half-dead creatures are packed densely together all the way to a distant hillside. Bodies of diseased, dead cattle litter the riverbank. As we watch, four men wearing only ragged shorts drag a fresh carcass to the edge, tip it over. It slides down, dislodges another carcass, and the two of them spill into the river together. The fresh carcass bobs to the surface, floats slowly away. The other one sinks.

During all of this I hear the steady click-click of Steph's camera, but I shoot nothing. I just watch. Silently.

It is almost dark when we see the glow. It doesn't seem far, seems to have flared up suddenly from the landscape. We look at each other through the gloom. Steph nods, and we press on.

It is a hill, the size and shape of a small volcano. The river disappears somewhere near its base. The glow from the top is orange. The smell is like sulfur ignited.

We scramble up the side of the hill. Stopping to rest halfway up, I see the ashes dancing in the glow up there, stirred, then settling, then stirred again.

Near the top, we slow, approaching cautiously. The night air is hot, but here, near the top of the burning mountain, it is hotter. Much hotter.

My face burns and I break into a hard sweat as I look out from behind the rocks, into the pit.

It is the size of a large stadium. And round—but ragged and uneven. On the far side, the trucks back up to the pit, one by one. The hiss of pneumatics floats through the cracking sound of the fire, and a truck's bed rises, its load falls. Tumbles down the molten side of the crater.

We work our way around, but I already know what we are going to find. I sense it, and I want to turn away, but know I cannot. We have come this far. There is no way to back out.

We stay in the shadows.

Both of us are afraid now. I have never felt fear like this before—knowing this is not the moment of our death, but the moment of all deaths.

As we draw near, we see the body parts. Arms and legs, hands, fingers, sticking out of the beds of the dump trucks. Then dumped and falling, the bodies twisting, gyrating in a fascinating dance down the hillside.

Steph is working her way around to get a better angle, trying to catch the truck and the bodies at once, with the glow rising from below.

I know she's gone too far, I can see the exact place where the dirt is weakening under the pressure of her foot—for a moment I am convinced I can actually hear the dirt crumbling—and I want to yell. I want to scream at her to get back, out of the light, into the shadows, where it's safe. I want to grab her and shake her and tell her *No more, no more of this!* It has gone too far and it is not a game and this has to stop now. This is it. The moment. The last moment.

But the words stick in my throat, my dry mouth, are held back by my cracked lips, and I say nothing. Her foot slips, and then she is sliding down the hillside.

I tell myself to move. Move! But my feet seem planted in stone, fused with the rock. And I watch her slip away.

THE DUNES

We drive east on 8, across the desert, screaming over hot asphalt in a truck. Soon we will cross the ugly brown trickle that once was the Colorado River. Before I was born. Before the dams and dumps. Back when nature did things on a large scale. Before we built our anthills quite so high.

We are returning to Arizona.

It is night. Hot night, and I have the gas pedal to the floor, the speedometer flirting with one hundred, the wind and dust battering the sides of the old truck.

She slides down on the seat, slips her legs out the window and snuggles her head into my lap. But we both know this is a fiction. She is not here. She didn't make it.

It's what my generation does. We watch things die.

It is long past midnight and the air blasting in the window is dry and hot. She shifts her head, nudges my belly, makes an uneasy noise. Her side is scraped where she fell against the rocky wall of the crater. My elbow is cut, my knee is bruised from lunging to the side, reaching for her.

Too damned late. The handcuffs are clamped on tight. I am impotent. There is just this burning inside—a superheated, acid-coated, diamond bullet piercing my stomach.

She reaches for me with one hand, strokes my forearm. I look down at her.

I feel the soft sink of tire in sand and the steering wheel jerks in my hand.

I look up. Too late. I press down on the brake pedal gently, grab the wheel hard with both hands. One of those little film canisters flies up from somewhere, pops open against the dash. The film pops out, unravels, floats out the window and is gone—a dark streamer in the night.

We are slipping now, and I feel the tire sinking deeper into the sand. Weight shifts as the front end loses momentum, slowing more sharply than the rest.

The moment yawns, the truck and the two of us hanging in the balance. I feel every bit of it now. I am one with the big steel beast, part of the machine. She is jerking upright, banging her head against the bottom of the steering column.

Then we stop.

I stumble out into the dusty haze. Look at the front end of the machine. It is not hurt badly. But it is tired. It will go no further tonight.

We are at the dunes.

I walk away from the truck, slogging up the sandhill. The moon is off to my right and very high and bright. Nearly full. I move at an angle to it. I don't want to walk right toward it—into it—I know that much.

The haze of dust seems to have followed me from the truck. I fall, slip, claw my way up the dune, then I am at the top and rolling down the other side.

I lie there in the sand for a while, panting hard. Then she catches up to me.

Together we stumble farther from the highway, deeper into the warm sand, over the hills. We can see nothing now but the stars and the great pale humps of sand. Rising, falling.

I stumble and she clutches at me, pulls me to my feet. We do not talk. I am winded. I lean down, hands on knees, gulping air.

I drop down into the soft, scratchy grains of sand, she settles next to me. I lay one arm across her. She reaches for me. Pulls my face to hers. She tugs at my shirt, pulls it over my head, and I unbutton her dirty jeans, work them down over her hips. Somehow we make love in the sand.

When we are done, she cries, and I don't understand why.

Enemies of Enormity
DAVID RIVARD

And thanks to a polymer the chemists jimmied-up in Bern
she can sweep a thin streak of blush across her cheeks
as any young woman might
if the spring is passing
as it is passing
through the well-advertised & transnational influence
of Chanel's "instant radiance to go"—
this skin of hers
a little skanky she almost thinks to herself
while staring in the mirror—
tho for this working girl & everyone else alive
today is a Tuesday a May 27th that no one can make behave
so that at the same time the girl is worrying her make-up
across the street in front of the post office
a panhandler in shorts is taking off his leg,
his plastic prosthesis unstrapped at the knee
its buckles bent & chafing, he holds his free hand cupped for coins
while the other rubs at the stump, absent mindedly stroking it
the way a man might the belly of his wife
if she were just three or four months pregnant,
that is to say, lightly,
his eyes inflected by worries, slight misgivings, fears,
but whose wouldn't be?
who wouldn't be afraid that the leg might be stolen?
it could happen, you could be distracted by a passing bus—
on the side of the bus a pin dropping in mid-air—
the pin imprinted there on the poster
the same pin
so often caught in the act of falling on a television screen
but in slow-motion

as it bounces on a glass table
by the mouthpiece of a white telephone
clarity is what's at stake it's said, who we are—
a light tap when the pin hits the glass—
and even if no one is sure that what they've heard
is what they were supposed to hear,
exultant or glamorous, precarious or sad,
they will all go ahead with what they have planned
for themselves
if only
it could be a moment when they stand unburdened
before this evening's bloody meats
tomorrow's thunderclap.

Persuasion
SHEILA KOHLER

He called M.'s house on the island the day before, in the hopes of finding her there, and got no reply. Now he is leaving the place. He puts down his heavy suitcase full of books which he has carried up the stairs onto the ferry, kisses his wife goodbye, and holds her slender body against his for a moment with regret. "Will you be all right?" he asks guiltily, knowing she cannot possibly be. She nods bravely and is gone fast in her gray, cotton dress.

He finds an empty bench and settles himself in with his suitcase, computer, and the book he carries in his hand, when M. surpises and delights him by suddenly appearing, it seems to him out of nowhere. He is not sure where she has come from or what she is doing here on this ferry which is going to the mainland so early in the morning. She greets him and sits down opposite him with the almost cat-like, yet careless grace of the famous and the privileged. She carries no baggage, though she has a heavy, bound book in her hand.

She apologizes for not returning his call, and he says rather rudely that it was probably better that way. He cannot really imagine her at his in-law's place. He thinks of their huge, white summer house on the hill with its vast and lonely view of sea and sky, the flowerless garden—"the bunnies eat everything," his mother-in-law has said, standing in her white, silk dressing gown on the terrace, a cup of black tea in her hand, gazing blankly into nothingness. In his mind's eye he sees the endless, elegant, anonymous rooms, with no knickknacks, no family photographs, no disorder of any kind, no flowers inside either, except for the one perfect orchid with its three large white blooms which has lasted four months, his mother-in-law has said, "almost as though it were not real." He sees the thick, white towels, all embroidered with the family initials in navy blue and the white deck chairs, with their thick, soft blue and white cushions, the narrow lap pool which is heated to such a degree, the steam rising from the water in the early mornings, that he has preferred to run along the narrow road in danger of being hit by a car, to find a rocky beach and the icy sea and to throw himself with relief into the seaweed and gray waves.

He imagines his in-laws, who are early risers, already eating their sliced grapefruit and prunes at this hour on the shiny granite table, his mother-in-law, her dark hair impeccably pinned at the back of her head, stretching forth a fine, trembling, white hand, to protest when his father-in-law, in a moment of inattention, dares to put down the orange juice carton on the breakfast table, while he sits on the bench on this ferry watching this woman sprawled effortlessly and elegantly before him.

He likes the way she looks at him directly, as he sits opposite her, as if she sees nothing else but him, her gray-blue eyes smiling, open wide, almost, it seems, without blinking. He hardly notices the ferry pulling away from the island, the pale blue summer sky, or the choppy, gray sea. He is looking at her, a youthful-looking woman, though she must be ten years older than he but with an air of innocence, he thinks, probably in her early fifties. She wears her hair almost shaved, which gives her a slightly surprised air, and her blue jeans with holes at the knees, though he knows she must be quite wealthy, perhaps even rich, surely, a successful film having been made from one of her books, he seems to remember, and probably many prizes won, and owning property on the exclusive island they have just left behind.

He knows some of her work and admires it, and he once read something she wrote about prayer which surprised and moved him. He knows, too, that she has recently received harsh criticism for a book, and he regrets now not having taken the trouble to read it and not being able to say something complimentary and kind.

She jumps up to go and buy her ticket and offers to buy his, too. Surely she is not going to pay for his, he thinks. Why on earth would she? He runs after her protesting, and finds she has only bought her own because he has followed her. There is a moment of confusion, before they sit down again face to face.

He mentions the teaching he knows she has just done, and she looks glad. He imagines she is pleased he has found an easy subject of conversation. Perhaps she, too, is thinking she has not read his first book of stories, or perhaps anything he has ever written and had published in various magazines. They talk about the difficulties of the teaching she has just done: the large classes, the student tutorials, and compare it to the teaching they have both done at another university. They mention some of the faculty and the head of the program whom they both like or are careful enough to say they do.

There is a pause, which she fills to his delight by asking what he is reading. After the last few days on the island with his wife's parents who never question him, or show interest of any kind in what he has done, or thinks, but talk when they talk at all of people, often famous dead people from their past, poets and painters, whom he doesn't know, or of their own various ailments or previous exploits, it is a delight and relief to have someone at least professing interest in what he might be reading. He holds up his slim volume of Jane Austen's *Persuasion* which lies on the wooden bench beside him.

"Ah, my favorite!" she exclaims, charmingly, he thinks, for he somehow takes her remark as a compliment to him, as though he had written the book. "Such a wise book and sad, in a way, don't you think?"

"The last book she wrote, though, *Northanger Abbey,* was published later—she died at forty," he informs her. He has recently read the excellent introduction to the book.

"Forty? So young, and she had written so much," she comments and smiles wistfully. There is something most endearing about the way she smiles, he thinks, the same simile coming to him again , the mouth curling up at the corners, like a cat in a cartoon—a most charming and accomplished woman, indeed, with such an air of sincerity and intensity. Or he, at forty, thinks of her as a charming and accomplished woman with an air of sincerity and intensity, though he realizes from her remark that she probably doesn't think of herself as that accomplished, though he knows how successful she has been.

He is only sorry he hadn't bothered to make more of an effort that morning, or to put on the smart khaki trousers he had considered wearing, instead of his rather grubby white pants and bluejean jacket when leaving the house on the island so early in the morning in order to escape it as soon as he could.

"Really, your favorite?" he asks and goes on to say that he has just reread *Pride and Prejudice* as well, and thought it so much better than the later book.

"But this one is really about persuasion while *Pride and Prejudice* is not really about pride and prejudice. It's about ... " she says and waves her rather stubby fingers in the air.

"Yes, you're right about that. It's about will Lizzie or won't she marry Mr. Darcy. And persuasion is a good subject. I've certainly been persuaded in my life, often enough, and sometimes against my will. Jane Austen's fiancé was persuaded not to marry her, apparently," he interrupts her to say.

"How sad," she says, and he nods and smiles, and thinks that really he likes everything this woman says.

He's delighted to have met her again in this way, without anyone else around, between lands, in a neutral zone as it were—such an intelligent woman and so nice, capable of intelligent conversation, someone who has actually read something. Having spent a week in his in-laws' summer house on the island where he had hardly been able to find a book which was not one of those large expensive glossy picture books about decorating, birds, or sailing, he feels no one really reads the way he does anymore—with the constant need for a book, rather like food or sleep or sex or at least a companion. For the hour-long ferry ride, he will be able to talk about what interests him most: books. He is able to forget for a moment that he is leaving behind his poor, defenseless wife to cope on her own with the usual assault of criticism from her parents.

"I don't like this steak. This doesn't taste like steak. It tastes like beef," her mother has said, wrinkling up her small nose, and pushing away her plate with the fillet mignon, after her only daughter has bought it, oiled and herbed it, and grilled it for her with care on the outside grill.

"It's only forty eight hours," he has told his wife, professing the dire necessity of going into the city to the library to consult his books.

Now he says he has been rereading all of Jane Austen in order to plunge into the mind, the conversation, even the language of the late eighteenth century, for a book he is researching, a historical novel about a woman who leaves France during the revolution and makes the sea crossing under great difficulties to escape the revolution.

She tells him that she is reading hundreds of books for a national prize and that oddly enough many of them are bad historical novels. "I'm not sure why—but you will do it well, as you are such an excellent writer," she adds even more charmingly. He shakes his head with modesty at this compliment about his writing but wonders then if his publishers will have sent his first book, a book of stories, for this yearly and prestigious prize, and if this adorable woman might have read it and might even feel inclined to include it in her list of suggested prize winning books, if she considers him such an excellent writer.

Really, he wants to get up and give her a hug or even a kiss on both her rather plump, rosy cheeks. He would like to pick her up—she's not very large—and put her on his lap or perhaps even sit on hers, he doesn't weigh much, and run his fingers through the stubble on her head. Instead it is she who rises and goes to the window to show him the nuclear submarine which is pulling up alongside the ferry, just the turret and the gray top emerging from the sea, with a few men standing precariously there. She explains that there is a nuclear submarine base nearby.

"Good God!" he says looking down at the large, menacing gray mass surging surreally through the water beside them. "I would last about five minutes in one of those," he says and puts his hand to his throat, imagining the cramped quarters, the lack of air, the constant claustrophobia. He doesn't like cramped quarters. She nods her head and laughs agreeably. Then she adds that there is one book among the many historical novels that she has had to read for the prize which he might like. It is also about France and the same period he is writing about. He wonders if it is the recent book by his friend Julian, and, indeed, this is the one she likes the best.

"Oh, I have read it!" he exclaims enthusiastically, clapping his hands together, when she mentions it. "He's a friend of mine, you know, and I think it's the best thing he's done. It seemed to me much freer and stronger somehow than some of his earlier work. I liked it so much. In fact he inspired me to tackle my own."

"Very good, isn't it!" she says with equal enthusiasm as they sit down again face to face, looking into each other's eyes with the mutual satisfaction of finding themselves in this intellectual agreement.

Then he thinks of Julian and what a prize of this kind would do to his career as a young writer. "And the book has been so unfortunate and received such horrible reviews," he protests on his friend's behalf loyally and vehemently, he believes.

"It did? Really?" she says incredulously.

"It got a horrid little In Brief in the *Times*," he informs her, which is true. However, he does not think to mention the glowing reviews in several other prestigious magazines and newspapers that he knows about. He thinks then that this may be just the sort of information which would make this decent, intelligent woman want to champion the book and give it the prize.

"How surprising," she says. And slyly she asks him what his friend is like.

What is he to say? he wonders. "Haven't you met him?" he asks, rather surprised, himself, for he imagines they move in the same circles.

She nods and confesses, "Briefly. He rather frightens me—so cool and elegant."

"He is elegant, isn't he?" And he thinks for a moment of Julian arriving at a party in white linen trousers and a transparent white shirt, shaking hands with people with a bored expression on his sharp face. He would like to add that his friend is rather cool and reserved, an intelligent, ambitious man whom he has seen less and less of as his friend's career has advanced. Instead, he says, "A very private person. I have known him for a long time, but I can't say I really know him that well." He adds quickly, "He's quite brilliant, of course."

"Yes, he would be," she says and looks at him and crosses her legs and smiles with what he takes for understanding. He's convinced this woman understands everything left unsaid as well as what has been said.

She looks out the window and tells him about the nuclear submarine station they are drawing near to at this point. "After 9/11 there were sharpshooters around here to protect the station," she says.

"Really. Good God!" he says again, amazed.

"How old is he, do you suppose?" she asks, reverting to their former discussion.

"A few years older than I—probably about forty-five," he says, adding on, perhaps, a year or two.

"Well, he's written an excellent book."

"Yes, it is—" he hesitates and cannot resist adding, "Though I must confess I got a bit bogged down in the middle bits with all the confusing different factions: the Jacobins and Jacobites and Girondins; the Mountain. I thought that went on for a bit too long."

"I haven't got to that part yet," she says and smiles.

When he leaves the ferry for the train he means to take into the city, she does not allow him to help her with her suitcase down the stairs. He puts this down to her age. Probably women of her age consider an offer to help an older woman with a suitcase insulting these days, he decides. Nor does she offer to drive him in her car to the station which is, after all, only a few feet away and probably more accessible on foot. They wave goodbye as she goes to her Mercedes, without having to go through the awkward business of shaking hands or even embracing. He calls out quite sincerely what a pleasure it was to talk to her. He walks off alone carrying his suitcase filled with books. He finds he is already swaying a little back and forth from the movement of the ferry which he had hardly noticed during the trip, and he sways even more when he hears his friend has won the prize.

Through the Apple Orchard
SEBASTIAN MATTHEWS

What can a boy do with such
information but store it in his body?
    —Robert Boswell, "Smoke"

All Alan wanted to do that last summer was go over to John's and smoke cigarettes with his friends. We'd wait until John's mom backed her car out of the drive—she had the late shift at the county hospital—then start rustling around in the pantry. If we got lucky, there would be a few cans of warm beer or some cooking sherry, and we'd kill the rest of the night up in his drafty barn loft out behind their ramshackle house, shooting the shit and listening to Zeppelin and Hendrix. The whole summer seemed to go that way.

In a few days we'd all be starting high school—Alan a Catholic school over in Concord, John the local public school, me all the way across the country. I couldn't have articulated the feeling then, but I remember the whole summer having this sense that something big needed to happen—that Alan and I had to make it happen—before it was too late. Before *what* was too late? I wasn't sure. Before the summer ended maybe, and with it my childhood. As if a screen door might somehow slam shut in the wind and mysteriously latch.

It made sense, then, when John's sister agreed to buy us a case of beer, to throw a big end-of-the-summer party. Made sense to hold it in John's loft, the perfect party spot. If Alan kept hanging on John's every word, following him around like a puppy, it wasn't like I had much choice. John and Alan called up everyone they knew, then John drove us to Concord in his beat-up Duster (though he only had a permit), his long hair whipping in the wind. We sat waiting in the New Hampshire state liquor-store lot for over an hour, paranoid about cops. I felt bad that we skimmed ten bucks off John's mom's stash, but John said he did it all the time, she never noticed, not to worry.

His sister finally showed, on her lunch break from Papa Gino's, sexy in her candy-red uniform. She had to pass alone under the new highway—her quick, staccato steps echoing inside all that concrete, signaling her arrival before we could make her out in the rearview. Then her pretty, other-side-of-the-tracks face there in the passenger's-side window, expression blank when she saw who was in the car.

"You're just kids," she said. Her name was Cindy or Sherry or something like that. "I shouldn't be doing this."

We laughed nervously. Alan fiddled with the radio knob. I had this terrific urge to lean forward and take Cindy/Sherry's face in my hands and kiss her. She looked at me like she guessed my fantasy and stuck her tongue out, darting it like a cat. Which was, in and of itself, almost enough. She got us the beer, though, and when John stepped out into the afternoon sun with a case in his arms, a shit-eating grin spreading full across his farm-boy face, I almost liked him, almost forgot that he was trying to steal my best friend. We hooted and hollered like we were at a rodeo.

I remember that drive back down the highway as one long rush of wind and blaring radio rock and roll. Little flashes of it filtering back. The cracked leather seat, the case of Narragansett under my arm, its cool cardboard pressing on my skin. John stiff-arming it down the highway. Alan turning back and smiling, crooning along with Tom Petty, *She's an American girl*.

John stored the beer in an old cooler full of ice while Alan and I pulled out all the best records. Styx. Kansas. REO Speedwagon. Aerosmith's "Toys in the Attic." I'd been listening to new music ever since the move, stuff John had never heard of or would ever like. Had been turning Alan onto my secret stash of New Wave 12" singles, some inner-city soul and prehistoric rap. But tonight it was classic rock all the way.

Alan and I tried to clean the place up, but it wasn't easy. John left his shit lying everywhere. I cracked Alan up by throwing a whole pile of John's shirts onto the floor. John walked right over them. So we went outside and made road signs out of old cardboard with magic-marker arrows pointing where to park. We knew we were acting queer; we just couldn't help ourselves.

Then, in a kind of stupid upping of the ante, we cancelled the party. Just like that. I forgot whose idiot idea it was. Probably John's. Either way, it was too late to call anyone—the windows already curtained with dark—so we just turned out the lights, crawled behind the couch with the beer and hid. Opened a few cans and started waiting for the world to go away. Every time a car drove in, we stifled our laughs and kept our heads low. People would yell up, stomp around a while, then get frustrated and leave. One group of John's friends actually climbed into the loft: four of them piling up the ladder. They had seen the signs and knew we were there but couldn't find the light switch.

"Pussies," John hissed.

Eventually people stopped coming, and we crawled out of our hiding place. By then we were piss drunk and amped up with adrenaline. Alan and I thrashed around in the dark, knocking over table stands and old lamps. We threw ourselves down on the dirty mattresses lining the walls as if enacting some wild ritual dance of hormonal joy. John flipped the light on and dared us to join him in drinking the whole case ourselves.

"Long live the Three Musketeers," he cried, and he and Alan threw up their arms in camaraderie, beer foam showering the floor.

I am not sure what I looked like standing there, but Alan threw me this furious glare. He started chewing on one of his shirt sleeves, like he did when we were kids. I knew he wanted me to join in, but I couldn't. Things were moving way too fast.

John said: "Let's go to Robin's!"

I was flipping through a stack of records and didn't respond, hoping the remark would pass unnoticed. But Alan nodded, which was enough for John. He climbed onto the old couch and shook his finger. He reminded me of my brother, always coming up with the plan, always commanding center stage. I felt a small jolt of sadness, a weird kind of pressure behind my eyes and in my chest; it seemed as if something was about to burst inside me and flood everywhere.

"We'll head east on Schultz's road," he said. "Walk until we hit the crossroads. It's a mile down the old logging road before we hit town." I thought, *no way*!

"A half-mile to the highway, three more to Pittsfield," John said, a lukewarm beer up at his mouth. "No problem."

He was drunk. Pittsfield was too far away to walk. Besides, his mom would get home and hear us sneaking out and know we'd been drinking.

"Good idea," Alan said, joining him in the center of the room.

"The town pump," John said, moving his arm up and down like a piston. "And I'm going to get me some water."

I made my way over to the trap door and started walking along its edge. My hands out like a trapeze artist, I tried to get close to falling but keep my balance.

John stomped over, knocking the beer out of my hand as he passed. The can spun to a stop, foam pouring out of its mouth.

"Fuck you," I said. "That's it for beer."

"Fuck you, too, Dubba!"

"Fuck you both," Alan said.

John's face lit up. He shouted, "Fuck! Fuck! Fuck!" and started dancing around the loft.

As John laced his shoes, Alan stared over at me again, the expression in his eyes, the posture of his body, shouting: "C'mon!" All I wanted was to go home, to talk back and forth across the dark room with Alan until we fell asleep. The way I saw it, we were sure to be caught. It was way too late for Robin to be up. Town pump or not. She'd be alone and scared to find three guys on her roof. Her parents would call the cops. But I wasn't going to admit any of that.

"Sure," I said, stepping down off the ledge. "Let's go."

What I remember most about that night is walking down the long dirt road, then passing through the apple orchard. How for a while there was only the sound of our feet crunching on the dirt, the *whoosh whoosh* of Alan's corduroys rubbing together. How my eyes eventually adjusted to the dark, and I could make out the far northern tip of Locke Lake through a stand of yellow pine; could almost picture the square of the dock out in the water, the moon drifting along the treetops like a buoy. How, later, we got separated from John.

And I remember all the times Alan and I shared on that lake: learning to swim one summer, then going for our lifesaver's license the next, joking around on the dock to impress the girls, even swimming across the thing once despite the shouts drifting out from the shore. We treaded water to get back our wind, out where the water was an impossibly dark blue. We laughed wildly, proud of ourselves, singing loud enough for anyone to hear.

The previous summer I had insisted we see *The Deer Hunter*. It was my fifteenth birthday, and I badgered my mom into taking us to the old theater off the Portsmouth circle. I can picture it clearly: coming out for intermission (they still had them then) as if we were the ones helicoptered out of our lives into the heart of Vietnam, fast-forwarded into men. As if me and Alan were the ones working side by side at the factory, then out in the wilderness together, silently stalking up through the trees, rifles materializing in our hands. I can remember just standing there looking at each other, shell-shocked, sipping our Cokes mutely until the lights blinked us back into the theater.

And I remember how we kept walking down that road, until it was way past midnight and we started getting cold. How I was about to suggest heading back when out of the blue Alan turned to me, an intense look on his face. He must have been thinking about *The Deer Hunter* because what he said could have come right out of it.

He said: "Some people have it and some don't."

He was staring right at me like he expected a reaction.

"Run that by me again," I said.

"Some people have *it*, but most people don't."

John leaned over, anger flaring up in his face. I could tell he didn't know what was going on.

"I see," I said. I thought I had it but wasn't sure.

"You and me've got it," Alan said.

Then I got it. "Like 'one shot'," I said.

Alan nodded his head slow and serious. That's what the two friends talked about in the movie. Just one shot to kill the deer. Nothing wasted. Alan nodded even harder. I looked sidelong at John, and I could tell Alan knew what I was thinking.

"But John don't," he said.

I started to nod but stopped myself.

John leaned over and gave me a push. "Shut up!"

Fuck *him*! He didn't get it.

"Tony Perez has it," I said. Perez was my favorite player.

"Yaz has it." Alan said. Yazstremski was his.

"Reggie Jackson has it," John said.

Alan and I laughed.

I said, "Reggie Fuckhead *thinks* he has it." This cracked Alan up. Reggie Jackson was way too full of himself.

I liked this game. And I was glad when John fell back a good twenty yards. I could hear him chucking rocks into the woods.

Alan said: "Mike and Willy have it, even though they're jerks." We had spent the summer avoiding our older brothers.

I nodded. "Your dad *wants* to have it. And my mom has it, but isn't sure."

Alan's hands were out in front of his body, palms grasped together, and he looked a little crazy. I was glad to be his friend. We went down the list of people we knew, putting them either in the "has it" or "doesn't" category. Tony, the only black kid in town, had it. And so did Freddie Morse, the boy with the tube in his head. Marie and Nadine had it for sure (and we wanted it).

Alan wanted to go get John, but I wouldn't let him. No way.

"Let him be," I said. I wished the road would go on forever.

Over the years this story has taken on a mythic cast: *the lost boy teetering at the threshold of young adulthood.* I can't seem to help myself. Every time I start to tell it, the story swerves into allegory. I don't know anymore what is true, partly true or pure fantasy. If that boy is even me. Does it matter? I am trying to pinpoint a feeling here, a tangible sense of loss.

A few basic truths.

1) It had been three years since I last lived in Barnstead. My brother and I following my dad around, moving to a new school each year, visiting Mom in the summers. I had to keep building anew my friendship with Alan. This was the first summer I had to contend with John.

2) When my mom left her boyfriend, Arthur, she moved into a walkup apartment in Portsmouth, three towns over. She lived over the local pub, The Press Room, where she met Charter, a Zen Buddhist anarchist wearing a *Gravity Never Sleeps* T-shirt. She followed him out to his hand-built house in an old hippy commune beside a swamp, deciding that night never to leave. I liked it, too, with its unruly vegetable garden and outhouses and long dirt roads, slowly warming up to Charter's stern but friendly presence. But I wanted to get back to my old life with Alan. Wanted to reclaim that feeling of endless possibility we always seemed to move within.

What else? The summer came to its abrupt close soon after that night. I moved back out to Seattle to live with my father. Alan and I saw each other here and there, a few times calling each other up out of the blue. But we grew apart in increments, in that casual manner of old friends who carry the implicit, naïve trust that the next time they hook up it will immediately feel like old times. As if whole blocks of a life hadn't passed between.

One more thing. For years, when telling the story to a roomful of friends at a party, I would leave John out of the story altogether. When

I finally put him back in—in my first clumsy attempts at writing this down—I'd have John get lost in the orchard or abandon us down by the schoolyard. I wanted Alan and I out there alone together on that highway. It makes sense that I wouldn't want John in the picture. If it's about anything, this story's about wanting things to stay the same. Wanting my brother to pay attention to me again. For my parents to get back together. For my father to stop moving each year. I wanted these uncertainties cut out of my life. Telling you this story now, I still do.

The way around the Lebrèque place was through the apple orchard. The house looming over the crossroads like a dilapidated sentry tower. By cutting through the orchard, we figured we wouldn't have to deal with Lebreque's killer German shepherd, King, who we knew from childhood tales was ferocious, most likely rabid, entirely evil. There was a hole in the property fence about a quarter-mile before the cross-roads and a ragged path through the apple trees that, if we could find it, would let us out far down the logging road, only a half-mile out of town. Alan and I had always gone through there.

The wind must have been heading straight for King, though. Even before the house was in sight we heard his deep bark. It stopped us in our tracks. Alan turned and shouted for John. No answer. He started to run back after him.

I grabbed Alan's shoulder and yanked him around. "C'mon!"

We broke into a run, side by side, arms pumping, running into the dark clutches of shadows reaching down at our heads. The cold air rushed past us. King's barking—I remember it as a mad, snarling howl—echoed in the trees. A feeling of exhilaration shot down my body like a vein of heat lightning. We were running together, my best friend and me. Alan turned once and smiled through a wild mask of fear. This had an eerie effect, as if he had died and turned into a ghost. I was his comrade, which made me a spirit, too. When the dark gap emerged in the trees on our left, a piece of the barbed-wire fence twisting back like in some movie, we plunged through it.

Alan and I must have lain on our stomachs like that for a long time. When we stood up we were sopping wet and cold. The wind had picked up and was howling through the branches above our heads. At this point we should have turned around and gone home. But something about the night—the coming end of summer, the impending separation, all that beer—led us forward, as if drawn forward by a magnetic pull into the heart of the apple orchard.

I remember Alan and I stumbling on, our hands before us, protection from low-hanging branches and the invisible cobwebs strung up like miniature clotheslines between the trees. How, moving around an apple tree, all of a sudden Alan was gone from my side. I called out his name, but the wind lifted my voice and pressed it down into the ground. I called out again, barely making out Alan's faint returning cry. I headed in that direction. The next time I heard his voice, fainter still, it was off in another direction. I was turned around. More than anything I didn't want to be in this stupid orchard, or in John's drafty shithole of a room, or even on the floor at Alan's. I wanted to be home.

The orchard was eerily quiet. I was worried that Alan had gone looking for John. That he might find him. And I wanted to know where that dog had gone. If he appeared out of the dark, I would climb a tree. I imagined Alan's dad, Mr. Yanski, out trolling for us in his old truck, his shotgun hung on a rack over his head and a Miller beer cold between his legs. He'd be angry as hell. I pictured my mother waking up with a dreadful intuition, afraid that I was hurt badly in a car wreck. I saw her passing nervously down the tilted hall, a glass of wine in her hand. I told myself that I had to find Alan, stay away from King, and find a way out of the orchard. I didn't give a shit about John. Let him freeze.

I walked for what seemed at least an hour, a strange feeling coming over me, as though I were passing up this long, scrolling hill that went on and on—as if I were walking the earth's curvature. If I kept going, I might see over the horizon into some new land. I knew that it wasn't possible, but there was something comforting in the illusion, and, for a few moments, I was an explorer, a lost hero making his way along the globe. Thoughts of *The Deer Hunter* resurfaced. The two friends separated by war. How they had to play that awful Russian roulette game to get out of the POW camp.

That made me sad and scared, so I started thinking back to the earlier scenes, to when the two friends were in their hometown just about to ship out for Vietnam, how they went out hunting together. I can't remember whether they bagged the deer or not. Maybe they let it go on purpose. I could almost see the deer darting away though the trees ahead of me. What I could remember was sitting in that theater wishing that they'd not have to go to war, that they could just stay together and hunt. But they get dropped into a sea of waving grass, dead bodies strewn around, and everything pushed down by this wall of helicopter noise and wind. Plumes of smoke rising from burned-down huts.

To cheer myself up, I remembered all the weekends I met Alan at the halfway point between our houses—out where the road switched to tar. If I got there first, I dropped my three-speed and stepped over the old stone wall that ran the length of Pitman's property. I was happy to wait among the pine and birch trees, content to rummage in the fern and dusty underbrush for phantom arrowheads. Soon enough I'd hear the scrape of pedals knocking against Alan's rusted-out bike frame, followed by heavy breathing, as he made it up the last few yards of the big hill, then the clatter of the bike being thrown down on gravel. He would be over the wall, suddenly beside me, and our long afternoon of adventure would begin.

I thought I heard a car on the dirt road, but its lights must have been off because there wasn't any light flashing on the trees. And it didn't sound like Mr. Yanski's truck—no rattle of tool chest knocking against truck cab. Only the thin, uneven hum of tires passing over dirt and gravel and the brief staccato rattling when the car passed over the river bridge. Then nothing.

The river bridge! Alan must have heard the car, too, and made the same crude calculations as I, because pretty soon I saw him up ahead, his arms out before him like a sleepwalker. I was chilled, worried for an embarrassing instant that King had gotten him, somehow transforming him into the walking dead. But then he saw me and ran my way. Together we made for the road.

Alan stumbled into the fence first. It was lucky he didn't cut himself on the barbed wire any worse than a few scratches on his hands. We moved along that ragged property line a while, eventually coming to a place where the fence had caved in under a fallen tree. I held the top wire gingerly between my thumb and forefinger, pressing down the middle and bottom wires with my shoe. By grabbing a branch, Alan got himself through. He did the same for me, and then we were on the logging road, only a short ways from town.

Alan kept saying that we'd run into John downtown, but I didn't think so. It was as if I had willed him out of existence. We walked with our heads down, pushed forward by momentum. The booze had worn off hours back. We walked and wished out loud that we had brought cigarettes. Looked for John by the stone bridge, then George Haller's Esso station, one solitary light on in the back. We looked for him at the center traffic light, but he wasn't there. We cut through the library's back parking lot and made for the schoolyard, standing in the middle of the soccer field and calling out John's name. Nothing.

Crouched out there in the cold, Alan and I talked about all the nights I slept over at their house. Big Mike getting drunk and terrorizing everybody. They'd never admit it, but all the Yanski brothers were afraid of their father. So was I. When Big Mike got going, their little house would be wired to blow. He'd settle in his Lay-Z-Boy chair after dinner and rule with the force of his stare, his unpredictability. His was a slow-burn anger that lingered underneath a smirking smile and placid eyes, a drunk's anger curled up like a rattler under a rock. We all sensed the silent rattle when the anger threatened. His fist pounding the kitchen wall, rattling the dishes. The screen door slamming behind him and the sound of his truck starting up.

I'd go to sleep in a sleeping bag wedged between Alan's bed and his big brother Mike's, a fluorescent Jesus tacked to the wall floating over me like some bad dream. Lying there in the dark we all wanted him to crash and, at the same time, would stay up waiting for the search beam of headlights to pass across the wall, for the slam of the truck door. The next morning everything would be normal, almost as if nothing had happened. Big Mike would go off to work or fiddle around contentedly with the Saturday chores, and we'd slowly ease our way back into our summer games.

One of us brought up that summer's Fourth of July fair. How we had hooked up with some older girls from Alton. We'd always tried to accomplish this feat, often pretending later that we had. Each year, as soon as Mr. Yanski found a parking space, we split off from the group and got lost in the crowd, free to roam the grounds for a few hours. We played carnival games and talked with friends from school, but most of our time was spent on the prowl. Would Nadine be there? Or Marie McCready, with her pretty Linda Ronstadt face? Maybe some new girl, her hair smelling of hay and saddle soap.

This time the two girls actually seemed to like us, and by midnight we'd sweet-talked them into coming with us to the graveyard. They stayed close to each other as we passed through the parked cars, whispering back and forth, splitting up as we passed into the front gate, the smaller one joining Alan. The skinny one with long blonde hair followed me to a nearby tree. She smelled like wintergreen Lifesavers, cherry lipstick. I held her close, not knowing what to say or how to make a move. She leaned against me, still and barely breathing. Then the fireworks were going off up in the sky. Alan's younger brother Kirk started calling our names from the parking lot, trying to get us back to the car before Mr. Yanski lost his cool. I was thinking that I had to kiss the girl or else Alan would have one over on me forever.

Eventually we gave up on John and went behind the school to look for butts. Lighting them in our cupped hands until the cold got to us. We agreed that it was time to start heading back. Which is exactly when John showed up. First a loud *whoop* out behind the playing field, then a shadow silhouette crossing like a ghost over the darkened grass, then John himself, larger than life, striding up with arms out.

Of course, John made fun of us for being afraid of King, who he had found tied up to a post, old and half-blind. And of course he wanted to keep going. We made three ragged loops around the school as we argued about it, passing through the basketball court, Alan and I swishing imaginary jump shots on the way out. Gradually, a vision of Robin's bedroom window shimmered back into sight. All we had to do was walk down the highway to get there—stride down the center of the street to the service road that would take us to Highway 14. It didn't matter anymore that we might wake somebody up.

When we got to the bridge, we dropped down to the small river trickling between the rocks. We used to hide there on skip days and had a little spot no one could find us in. Our outlaw hideout. We were standing in the stream, pissing, when Alan spotted the skulls. They lay in the dark water, glowing eerily among the rocks. Three cow skulls. One with big horns sticking out. I went in after them but couldn't get myself to drag them out. Something about putting a curse on us if they were moved. Alan made a lame joke, but we were too spooked. All we could do was poke at the skulls moodily with sticks and look into the empty eye sockets.

I need to stop for a moment and tell you something. It won't take long.

Last year I was out hiking on the mountains-to-sea trail, which up here runs parallel to the Blue Ridge Parkway, no more than half a mile from our home in Asheville, North Carolina. I'd been venturing down a side trail which turned into a narrow footpath that, after a few twists and turns, dead-ended in a small clearing. Before I knew it, I had stepped inside a small apple orchard. As soon as I was standing inside the rows of gnarled trees, I was teleported back to that night in the orchard with Alan. Scenes from it flashed in front of me like a waking dream. And have kept flashing with more or less intensity since. These days I go back at least once a week.

Often on these walks I try to make sense of that long-ago night. I bring pages of this story, folded lengthwise in my back pocket and pull them out when a new idea comes. Working this way, I often walk into the booby-trap webs the spiders spin across the path, stringy death masks forming to my face. (I must look like a caricature of a nature writer.) And you might not believe me when I tell you that a few weeks ago I discovered the entire orchard of trees yanked up by gnarled roots and dumped onto the ground. But it's true. Some sort of blight, I guess. But sitting there in the dirt, all I wanted was to stuff one of the bony roots in my bag, replant it in my yard. It felt like another blow, another thing I had no control over.

With the cow-skull visions in our heads, we climbed out from under the bridge. We stood around knocking the mud off our pants, and this little mutt of a dog appeared. Alan tried to pet it but the mutt kept backing up. I tried scaring it off by shouting and throwing rocks near it. But Alan got worried we might wake up the sheriff who lived down the street. The dog wouldn't leave us alone. We turned down Jenkins Road, doing our best to ignore it.

A street light sputtered out as I passed beneath, and that, too, felt like bad luck. I hurried up to catch Alan and John, who were passing down into an irrigation ditch. For a moment, all I could see was John's bushy head of hair peaking out over the embankment.

"Wait up," I called. "Let's keep together."

Not long after we reached the service road, we came to the outskirts of Pittsfield. The dim highway lights in sight. Our spirits lifted when we got out on the endless runway of tar: the open space eased the cold and fatigue that had overcome us. Everything had a majestic feel. If we have made it onto the highway, I thought, Pittsfield must not be too far away. Visions of a warm house rose inside me, temporarily easing the hunger pangs that cramped my stomach. I dreamed of a warm couch to sleep on, maybe something good to eat, the warm, sleep-fuzzy face of Robin floating at the door. John raised his arms above his head, started singing a song off the radio and kicking his legs out. I could understand what Alan saw in him, something of his wild spirit. He had brought us onto this highway. We had made it this far. Maybe we'd get to Robin's house, after all.

This is where things get spread out. Alan runs ahead, chasing after the dog, whistling for it. (Or maybe I'm just making up the dog.) Lost in my thoughts, I walk the road's center lines, doing my best to stay inside their little corridor. Like train tracks, only easier to manage.

"Stay on the side of the road," I yell after a car comes upon us unexpectedly, zipping past in a receding tunnel of hum. I stumble along in the grass and gravel. If only we stay a little off the road, I think, we will be okay.

Next thing I know, I am standing beside Alan hunched over on the side of the road. I think he's just out of breath. The moon's not in sight; the sky washed out gray.

"Ouch," Alan says softly, his hand up under his chin.

"What's wrong?" I ask.

"Ouch," he says again, staggering toward me. He has his hand in front of his face: keeps putting it up against his neck then holding it back out and looking at it.

"It's blood," he says. "It's fucking blood."

I place my hand on Alan's neck. When I take my hand back, I have slipped a glove on. Alan's bleeding badly.

John walks up.

He says, "Get up, you pussy!" before realizing Alan is hurt.

"Shit, Alan," he says. "You're fucked up."

Alan looks at me, back at his hand, then up at John. He touches his neck again and looks blankly at John.

"No shit, Sherlock."

I'm about to cry.

"He ran into something," I say, just before Alan slumps into my arms. All I can do is lower him to the ground.

The reflector post Alan ran into stands a few yards off the side of the highway. You wouldn't see it unless headlights lit up the diamond-shaped metal in a glint. Alan sliced his neck open along its crude edge.

I take off my sweatshirt and press it to Alan's neck. I'm kneeling over my friend, rocking myself back and forth out of nervousness. John crouches behind me.

"Somebody call an ambulance," I say to myself, knowing as I say it that it's a stupid thing to say. Alan tries to get up; I hold him down. *Oh fucking God*, I think, *he's going to die*.

"I need to get to the hospital," Alan mutters. "I need to get to a hospital."

"You'll be okay," John says. He stands up and runs to the road. Then he walks back, stands over us, arms wrapped around his chest, rocking.

Alan tries to sit up again, and I have to struggle to hold him. Despite all the blood loss, he's manically strong.

"I'm okay. I can get myself to the hospital. I feel fine. I can run to the hospital."

I have to laugh. It's the shock. He's all nerves and adrenaline. He's looking at me but through me, doing everything he can to break free.

"Shut up, asshole!" I yell, pressing the drenched sweatshirt even harder. This makes Alan moan.

"I'll go get help," John says. He's ready to bolt.

"Just stay still." I am talking to Alan, but John stays where he is. (Or maybe it's John who says this and me who is ready to flee.)

Alan's energy starts to run down, and he settles into an uneasy sleep. I sit with him like this for a while. John joins me. We watch the sky turn almost white. A haggard flock of birds cuts a path through the sky, a flimsy arrowhead disappearing over the treetops. I remember asking John to go for help. If Alan is going to die, I want to be alone with him. But that's a lousy thing to do. John runs all the way into Pittsfield, and Alan dies anyway. We both stay there with Alan. Somehow, everything will be okay.

I have been walking and writing again. A morning jaunt through this now familiar forest; heading back to the newly planted orchard. I have stopped to jot a note. It's about, of all things, *On the Road*, which I have been rereading for one of my seminars. In a passage late in the book, Sal and Dean are older, their friendship already tested by the years. They've just been schooled in a pick-up game by some youths and are heading back to a coldwater flat. They toss the ball back and forth between them playfully, improvising a little dance of togetherness. I write in the margins: *this is it*. Then underline "it." What am I getting at? Is *It* the love men share when they slip back into being boys? Or is it the feeling best friends have for each other when they step together into that peculiar fantasy of growing up? I don't know.

All I know is that I want to tell this so full that the story bursts all over itself. For you to see without me having to tell you that the whole thing is really about my brother. Even though he only pops up in the story here and there. That I never tell you what he looks like or the shitty things he did to me just so he could feel superior. When I look up, I don't recognize the way. Must have turned down a side path. Almost turn back but then keep going, following the leaf-strewn trail over a trickle of stream and up to the other side of the orchard. Even though this is a new route, I know exactly where I am.

Half an hour later, I am back at the bottom of the hill, *On the Road* tucked in my back pocket. It's funny. Reading this familiar book of my young adulthood, after all these years, I find myself on a trail both old and new, simultaneously the right direction and off course. Like with *The Deer Hunter*, how the De Niro and Walken characters became larger-than-life versions of us up on the screen—the unspoken connection they shared in the woods during that first hunting trip embodying our own friendship. They had *it*. And how in this story I am both the twelve-year-old heartsick boy pulled from his mother for the first time and the fifteen-year-old teen yearning for the distracted love of his father. In both, the hero has fallen in love with his friend, a spirit brother. In both, he gets lost in the dark heart of being alone.

We hear the police car coming before we see it. Humming like in a dream, it pulls up directly behind us, headlights flicking off. The patrolman steps out, looking weary, as though he has just come from a funeral. He crouches down and takes Alan from my arms. I must have slipped into shock because I'm not able to get up for a while. Then Alan is up on the hood of the car, and the cop has me hold down his legs. He tells Alan not to move, that the important thing is not to move. The cruiser's hood is warm and the engine underneath clicks as it cools down. Then the cop radios in.

It takes the ambulance a long time to come. In that eternity I must tell Alan a hundred times not to move. Finally, I hear the siren and see the flashing lights play along the electric wires. The cop is over talking to John. Alan has fallen into a half sleep. I stand suspended over him forever. Then two men lift the stretcher and take Alan away.

I remember the cop asking us if we have been drinking. John starts to lie, but I tell him the truth. We've been drinking a lot. I expect him to lecture us on the evils of alcohol, but he doesn't say anything except that he thinks Alan will make it. I thank him, as if his saying it is going to make it true.

We get in the patrol car, and the cop drives us back to John's house. I wanted to ride by Alan's side in the ambulance, to stay with him through the morning, but they don't let me. I go to bed on John's cold loft floor instead, lying there in the dark wishing I am anywhere but where I actually am. That Alan is okay and I'm not going away.

The rest of it gets blurry. I've been told that my step-dad, Charter, came and got me the next morning. But, I must confess, I remember Mr. Yanski coming for me, as though it were still the summer after fifth grade, as though my mom had never sent us away to live with our father, as though we had never left Barnstead.

In my fantasy, I am on my own, walking around John's cold room looking for my socks. My mother is still unreachable. The remnants of the previous night are strewn everywhere. I am sick with sadness. Eventually, I get myself down the ladder and outside to find a thin layer of fog draped over the top of the grass. Mr. Yanski is sitting in his idling truck, strangely quiet, almost serene, with a pipe clenched between his teeth the whole ride. I want him to tell me stories about his wild childhood or his stint in the Navy, but he just sits there quietly and sucks on his pipe. When we pass off the blacktop onto the dirt road, the tires bumping into the tops of the wells, I start crying. I imagine Alan alone in that hospital bed, tubes in him, machines blinking. I think of going to Seattle, to a big high school without Alan. I try to picture my brother inside the house, but he has already moved out. Mr. Yanski doesn't say anything or try to stop me. The tears dry up before we get to my house.

The lights are on in the kitchen. My mom must've been waiting for me all morning. When the truck comes to a stop, Mr. Yanski leans over to open my door and gives it a hard push. I can smell his cheap aftershave, and his pipe, his sweat. I slip out of the seat, turning back to wave goodbye. The truck has already started backing up, so I go into the house.

Those Moments
RICHARD GARCIA

The sky this evening over Charleston,
just dramatic enough to say, it's good—
strolling across the parking lot while the sun
lights up the bottom of clouds as you
are on your way to Taco Bell. Those clouds
remind you of a tromp-l'oeil crepuscule
in Las Vegas that makes you believe
you are sitting by a canal in Venice
in the early evening. The gondoliers
in their striped shirts drift along the shore.
O Sole Mio. The sky nostalgic, wisps of cirrus
seem to drift across it. You ask to sit outside,
because this is one of those moments, even if this
is not Venice, even if you're really indoors.

Locked Out
ALISON LESTER

It was by far the hottest summer in the three years we'd been in Tokyo. I couldn't go out without feeling unequal to the challenge of getting back home. Even when I put the air conditioning on in the apartment, I could still hear the relentless mating calls of the cicadas outside—like chainsaws in a rain forest—reminding me of the intensity beyond the windows. Children went by in the mornings, dragging their feet and perspiring. I couldn't wait to see them skip and scuffle again in the fall. And what must it have been like for really old people? Every morning, all spring, there had been a woman across the road who pulled the few dozen hairs she had left into a tiny bun at the back of her head, opened her sliding door, put down a mat, and knelt to weed with chopsticks in her tiny garden of potted flowers. I hadn't seen her in weeks.

There were Sundays when it was almost too hot for our favorite weekend treat of crêpes in the Omotesando area of Tokyo. Some Japanese like to say that Omotesando is like the Champs Elysées in Paris. I don't know what they're talking about. Omotesando is shorter and narrower, and most of its charm is hidden in its side streets.

This was one of those hot Sundays. We had settled ourselves at Le Bretagne, and had been served our usual order of galettes complete with cider when Hank said, "The people in the office think I'm sleeping with Ikeda-san." He related this as if it was supposed to be funny, but it was amazing how simultaneously my face felt hot and my heart felt cold. Maybe it wouldn't have been so bad if Natalie, who worked at Louis Vuitton, hadn't told me just the day before that her company's French president had given his rather severe wife the heave-ho in favor of a sparkling Japanese sales manager.

"Oh?" I said, forking some warm cheese and ham into our three-year-old son, Miller.

"Can you believe that?"

"Maybe," I said.

"She's a bit of a flirt, you know."

97

I looked at him. "I didn't know." Miller was losing interest in his food, so I let him shake some salt on it.

"Yeah," Hank continued, sitting back with a fresh cup of cider, easing into his story. His big, boyish face belied the way his broad chest and thick arms made him look prepared for anything. "When she started she was making one of the other guys really uncomfortable by bringing him tea every morning and standing on tiptoe to adjust his tie and stuff."

"I thought that was their job."

"Not in foreign companies it isn't."

"That's good to hear."

Hank didn't seem to register the chill in my tone—he's used to me being a little sarcastic—and continued his story.

"Yeah. So when she came over to me I told her she was being unprofessional."

"Can I play with the shoes, Mommy?" Miller asked.

"Sure, sweets," I said, wiping his face. He slid off his chair and headed for the wooden clogs artfully arranged in the corner of the room. "How'd she take it?" I asked Hank. I wasn't sure I was enjoying the conversation, but I was always quite fascinated by the ways Japanese women worked things out for themselves.

"She definitely looked shocked," he said. "And a little huffy. I guess I caused her to lose face."

He dug back into his food with enthusiasm, but I wasn't ready to do the same. "So why the rumor?"

"What?"

"Why do people think you're sleeping with her?"

"It gives them something to do?" he suggested.

I looked at him skeptically over the rim of my cup. "She's not even that pretty."

Hank looked very surprised to hear this, but then seemed to correct himself. "Look," he said, "she's only twenty-two. Her father probably never talks to her, her mother's probably a grin-and-bear-it housewife. She's had no one to teach her how to behave in an office."

"Until now," I said, and we both looked out the window rather than at each other. On the sidewalk, a pair of well-dressed Japanese women with little designer handbags over their forearms wondered whether or not to brave this foreign restaurant. They caught sight of us staring at them and skittered away.

Hank shook his head. "It's just getting a little weird again. I think I'll try to find her a mentor."

We heard Miller shouting "I don't *like* you!" to someone in the corner, and Hank got up, leaving me alone with the dregs of my cider and a heart he had set spinning like a penny.

There was too much come and go for me in Tokyo. It took the first nine months to find Melitta, a German woman Miller and I met in a nearby playground. She and I used to have tea together a few times a week and share Japan survival tactics. When she had trouble during her second pregnancy, I looked after her little boy for a few days. It began to feel like I was living in a neighborhood rather than just on a street. But her husband's job suddenly took them to Paris. We wrote for a while, but then she had a third child.

I liked Natalie, but she worked all the time. The women at the American Club—a sprawling complex cheek-by-jowl with the Russian Embassy where we could laugh with our mouths wide open, order club sandwiches, put up signs when we wanted to sell our king-size comforters or exercise bicycles—were friendly and energetic, but since they always seemed to be striving so hard for their grim smiles, I didn't want to rain on their parades. There was a beautiful young Japanese woman living upstairs from us with her husband and two little boys, and sometimes I thought we could be friends. We were always meeting in the echoing marble entrance and calling to each other that we should get together soon (her English was letter perfect), though we hardly ever did. The one time she did manage to come by, I sat and envied her hair, her clothes, and her face, while she told me about the PhD she was hoping to do someday on the Japanese attitude toward Jews. I don't remember what brought it on. She just seemed to be bursting with it, as if it were some sort of confession. I wasn't sure I could do that again.

A Korean family moved in next door sometime that spring. The wife's name was Sook Young. I only remembered because I made her write it down for me, and had stuck it up on the kitchen wall. When I first saw her, with her heavy long hair pulled up and her mules and trendy dress, I immediately thought *bimbo*. She was unusually leggy, unusually voluptuous, and her fingers were long and strong. Soon afterward I heard the most beautiful music coming through her front door. It turned out that *she* was singing it. *And* playing the piano.

Our kitchens were right next to each other, and every evening I heard her chopping away like crazy. Once I went over to see if she could spare an egg. She came to the door in an apron, with a shiny, sweating face and strands of hair like careless strokes of calligraphy on her cheeks and forehead. Her smile was so sweet, it was like one of those Japanese cartoons.

"Wow!" I said when Miller and I followed her into the kitchen. I was making a quiche, which I thought was pretty fancy until I saw what Sook Young was preparing. She'd just fried some chicken and placed it on a glass plate lined with lettuce. I could smell rice cooking. There was a salad and something dark green and fermented-looking already on the dining table.

"What are you making?" she asked me.

"Quiche," I answered.

"What is quiche?"

"Oh, it's kind of a cheesy pie. Eggs, milk, cheese, vegetables, maybe a little bacon or salmon. In a pie crust."

"And?"

"And?"

"Just quiche?"

"Yeah, just quiche."

She sighed. "You are so lucky."

"I am?"

"If I no put many dishes, my husband very unhappy. Is. Is very unhappy."

I studied her flushed face. "Every day?"

She nodded, sliding hairs away with the back of her hand.

"Yikes," I said.

She laughed and rubbed Miller on the head. She opened the fridge, releasing an aromatic cloud smelling of cold garlic, dried chili, and something between ginger and dirt. She found me an egg and slipped a chocolate into Miller's hand.

Back in our apartment, I tried to doll up my quiche with a ring of cucumber slices around the edge of the plate. I did feel lucky not to have to sweat it out in the kitchen for so long every night. People everywhere paid so much more attention to detail than I did—the ash around the eyes, the bamboo stake through the lip, the beads and shells, the lingerie, the deliberate contrasts. You would never see a matched set of porcelain at a Japanese meal. Each plate or bowl was chosen for the way it suited the dish or tidbit being served. I could hardly look at my wedding china anymore, it was so monotonous. And when a woman put on a kimono, the obi she tied it with had to be made not only in a contrasting design but also of a contrasting fabric. Meanwhile I went around in navy slacks and a white shirt, and sometimes I remembered to change my earrings.

I saw Sook Young again on the following Saturday morning. I'd taken Miller out for a spin around our block of tightly packed apartment buildings on his tricycle. People rose late on the weekends, so there were few cars about. Sook Young was coming in from grocery shopping. I'd seen her husband driving off in a champagne-colored Jaguar earlier.

"Was that your car?" I asked her after I mentioned seeing him.

She shook her head. "Company car. My husband is playing golf with his boss."

"I see," I said. "That explains the amazing green shirt. Does he play a lot of golf?"

She thought for a moment. "Golf," she said. "Golf is . . . Golf is the other woman."

She smiled, so I laughed. "I guess having the Jaguar to drive on the weekends is no compensation."

It took her a little while to understand this, but then she nodded repeatedly. "No compensation," she said, enjoying the word. She said it again. "No compensation."

It was so easy to tell Hank I loved him. "Love you," we always said at the end of a call if I phoned him at the office. Another woman might have told her husband in the middle of sex, to increase the tenderness of the event, but I knew Hank didn't like to be interrupted. He was very hearty about his lovemaking, in a charming, prehistoric way. That night, though, he started to talk.

"You know what I like, Cath?" he asked between deep breaths, snatching me back to the present from a reverie about a high school biology teacher.

"Tell me," I replied warmly, astounded and aroused by this new intimacy.

"Slippers," he exhaled back.

"What?"

"Slippers," he said again. The word had apparently flipped his switch and he was thrusting again.

Before we fell asleep I turned to him. "Slippers, Hank?"

"Never mind," he said.

"What kind of slippers?"

"Forget it, okay?"

Hank's attention was in short supply in Tokyo, since he was so motivated about his work. We'd sit down to dinner and I'd see him shake his head a little as he lifted his fork. Sometimes his lips even moved.

"Who are you talking to?" I'd ask him, and he'd smile, but it wasn't enough to bring him all the way home.

So one morning, when it was clearly going to be unbelievably hot, I pulled out the shorts I'd been wearing when we met, and put them on. I was already wearing my bathing suit, in anticipation of doing some laps at the American Club, but I had yet to throw on a top. I went out to the kitchen where Hank was making his morning coffee.

"Hey," I said.

"Hey," he said back, then did a double-take.

"Aren't those—?" he asked.

"Yeah," I said, smiling and doing a turn for him.

He poured his coffee, then looked at me again. "They're getting a little old, don't you think?" he said.

"What do you mean?" I asked. I should have said yes. No, I should have said no and shut him up. Instead I had to ask him what he meant.

"Well, they just seem to have lost their shape a bit, that's all," he said, sipping. "Why don't you go out and get yourself a new pair?"

Ha ha. He had no idea what it was like for an American woman of average size to shop in a city like Tokyo. I was a size 10 at home, a perfect M in my opinion, but in a country where clothes were made for laxative-popping secretaries (excuse me, *assistants*) like Ikeda-san, I was huge. I'd been an extra large for three years.

"Fly me home," I told him.

"What?"

"Japanese clothes don't fit me, Hank. Not to mention the fact that they're ugly."

"They're not all ugly," he said.

"No? Where've you been shopping?"

"Come on, Cathy, this is a huge city. There must be something big enough for you in it."

"I have better things to do with my time."

"Fair enough," he said, setting his coffee mug in the sink. This was office speak   how he talked to his employees. In his mind, Hank had already hit the road.

He kissed me on the cheek when he left, but kissed Miller on his Rice Krispie-flecked lips. I tried not to let it bother me, but it did. Poor Miller found out just how much when he went and poured himself some more apple juice just for the fun of pouring, then refused to drink it, right before we needed to leave the apartment to get him to daycare.

"Drink it," I said.

He didn't move a muscle.

"Drink it," I said again, enunciating with menace.

He was a statue, staring at the table. Very impressive.

I picked up the little green cup and held it in front of his mouth. I should have softened here, but felt myself make the choice to go on. "If you aren't going to drink it," I told him, "don't pour it!" I slammed the cup back down on the word *pour*. The apple juice jumped up out of the cup and splashed onto Miller's shorts. The ball I was trapped in started rolling faster down its hill. I pointed to the front door. "Go and get your shoes on," I ordered.

Miller looked down at his wet shorts.

"Go!" I shouted. "Hurry up!" I pulled him out of his chair and pushed him toward his shoes. When I got him there he finally started wailing in disbelief. He had a point. I hardly ever shouted at him. But I was lost, and started shoving his shoes on his feet.

"But my shorts are all wet, Mommy!" he sobbed. "I'm all *wet*!"

"And whose fault is that?" I hissed back. When I looked at his face I could see that he had quite logically worked out that it was my fault, so I quickly pressed on. "Okay, okay," I said resentfully, dragging his shorts down and unbalancing him so he had to put his hands on my shoulders. I should have hugged him then. Instead, I got up and left him standing alone by the door in his little Thomas the Tank Engine underpants, and went to get him some clean shorts.

When I returned his face was wet with tears and snot was creeping toward his top lip. I pulled the clean shorts on over his shoes and grabbed a tissue from the bathroom.

"Blow," I commanded, holding the tissue over his nose. He wouldn't. His big brown eyes stared at me. Tears had pulled his long eyelashes into shiny stars. "Blow," I said. "NOW!" We glared at each other. Part of me wanted to whack him so hard. Another part knew I should cuddle him and bleat apologies. Yet another part had nothing but admiration for his defiance in the face of my uncontrollable rage. I was desperate for him to obey me, but then again I would have hated for my little boy to be afraid of me. The hell with it, I thought, and stuck the tissue in my waistband. I reached for his backpack, shoved my feet into flip-flops, and pushed him out the door.

When it clicked behind me I realized I'd left my keys inside.

"Oh no," I said.

Miller blinked. "What, Mommy?" He could tell I wasn't focused on him anymore, and looked hopeful.

"I left my keys inside."

"That's okay," he said.

"Sure. Except that I can't get back in, can I?"

"Oh," he said. "Oh no."

I deserved to be locked out. "Silly Mommy," I said.

Miller knew this was his key to smile again. "Silly Mommy!"

"Silly Mommy getting so angry she can't remember her keys." I picked him up and put him on my right hip, with his backpack over my left shoulder. "I'm so sorry, Miller," I said with my nose right up against his cheek. "I got too angry."

"That's okay," he said. "*Now* I'll blow my nose."

People simply did not walk down the streets of Tokyo—even the back streets—in bathing suits and shapeless shorts. This wasn't a terribly serious problem for me, though, since everything foreigners did was considered relatively strange. You could see it in their faces as you passed. It was like they were thinking, "That's *weird*! Oh, wait, she's a foreigner. Figures." Every once in a while you'd see a flash of "I wish I could do that" in their eyes, usually if it was winter and you'd put on a nice warm hat. This was a country where, not so long ago, they walked around all year in sandals and two-toed socks. When it snowed, they put the sandals on stilts. Drier, but still cold. So walking back home from the daycare center in a Speedo wasn't a problem for me. What *was* embarrassing was standing outside my building with no keys.

I pressed Sook Young's buzzer, desperately dragging the depths of my brain for the correct pronunciation of her name.

"Oh!" she exclaimed when she saw me on the video intercom.

"I'm locked out," I said. "Can you let me in?"

"Yes," she said, and the doors slid open.

"Wait!" I shouted into the speaker, worried that she thought this was all I needed. "Can I come to your apartment?"

I heard her laugh. "Of course."

When she opened the door she laughed again, gesturing for me to come inside. Sometimes her English deserted her completely.

"May I use your phone?" I asked.

She pointed, then sat down to watch me.

I called Hank. I told him what had happened and said, "You've got your keys, right? Can I come and get them?"

"Sure," he said. Then he added, "Wait, let me think. Would it be better for you if I put them in a cab and asked the driver to take them over?"

"Too risky," I said. There were almost no such risks in Japan, but I wanted to inject myself into his day and get a better look at Ikeda-san. I wasn't going to let the opportunity slip away. "I'll be there in about a half hour."

"You have money?" he asked.

"I'll get some." Sook Young was smiling in such a friendly way that I knew this was true.

"See you in a bit, then," he said, and we hung up.

Sook Young sat up straight, as if ready for whatever I was going to say next.

"Can I take a shower?" I asked her. I'd worked up quite a sweat.

"Of course," she said, getting up.

I stood as well. "Can I borrow some clothes?"

She smiled. "Yes."

"Can I have some money?"

She laughed outright. "Anything," she said.

While I was in the shower, hoping that the woodsy-smelling goo I was putting on my hair was shampoo, she pulled out some clothes for me. She may have been Asian, but she was my size.

"You need underwear?" she called through the door.

"Um, actually, yes. Do you mind?"

In answer, the door opened a little bit and her hand came in, depositing a couple of lacy white garments on the edge of the sink. It entered again with a towel, then withdrew, at which point I stepped out and dried myself. Wrapped in the towel, I picked up her hairbrush, which was full of her long, unbelievably strong black hairs. This made me think of Ikeda-san. Her hair must feel like this, I thought. If Hank was having an affair, I could imagine strands of it between his thumb and index finger. Not pale brown (or, let's face it, occasionally white) like mine, but black and heavy and musky and young. I clawed Sook Young's hairs out of the brush and dropped them in the little plastic trash can.

When my own hair was brushed, I unwrapped myself from the towel and pulled on the panties Sook Young had chosen for me. I put my arms through the bra straps and leaned over to drop my breasts into the cups. Standing up to do the hook, I had a shock. I was beautiful. "Is it okay?" Sook Young asked from beyond the door, which was still a little ajar.

"I look fabulous!" I called back and opened the door to step out.

"We are the same size!" she exclaimed, handing me some shorts and a light blue knitted top. "Don't worry," she added. "The underwear is new."

"Do I look worried?" I said, pulling on the very cute khaki shorts. "Where did you buy them?"

"Isetan," she said. "Very cheap."

I loved this. Most people in Japan didn't like to talk about how cheaply they bought stuff. In fact, according to Natalie, despite the still-struggling economy, Louis Vuitton had never done better.

I pulled on the top, and we both looked at me in the mirror of her vanity table.

"I feel like I'm in college again," I said.

She smiled and nodded at my reflection. "I'm never bored with you." She handed me a five-thousand-yen bill at the door. I couldn't bring myself to borrow shoes as well, so I put on my flip-flops and went out into the heat.

In the back of the cool taxi I felt like a million bucks. In my mind I was full of youthful irresponsibility, and I was on my way to surprise my boyfriend. I planned how I'd step into Hank's office, turn my back on his busy colleagues, and flash him a view of the lacy bra I was wearing.

When we arrived I got out of the taxi, laughed at the ugly clothes in the window of the designer boutique—Hanae Mori just wouldn't quit it with the bias cuts and the butterflies—and got in the elevator. The blood in my body felt like sap rising. I breezed past the uniformed receptionist, walked down the hall and turned the corner. Hank saw me through his window and nodded at me to come in. When I opened the door I saw that he was talking to Ikeda-san.

Even though she was reclining in her chair, her back was poker straight, pushing her little apple breasts up and slightly out of her fancy black tank top. Her hands gripped the arms of the chair, and her legs were crossed. The tension in the room made it hard to breathe. Hank looked like a coil of steel.

"Here's the other woman I sleep with," he said to Ikeda-san.

He thought he was joking, but I didn't laugh and Ikeda-san didn't move a muscle. She kept looking at him as if he were going to tell her what she should do. There was definitely some satisfaction in watching him struggle between wanting to guide Ikeda-san in the right direction and wondering what I was going to do as I towered over her. I considered breaking her arm, not because I thought she had seduced my husband—I wasn't sure about that—but because it would have been so easy to do. I feel the same way about Chihuahuas.

"Nice to see you again," I finally said, holding out a hand in a way that would force her to stand up to shake it. I could have bowed slightly, and she could have bowed back, but I thought she should get up.

She did. "Nice to see you again, too," she said, and we shook. Her hand was limp and cold and damp, and submitted to the force of mine as if it were holding its breath and praying for deliverance. How could this person have been attractive? Why was submission better than enthusiasm?

At this point I knew that, having performed our ritual, we were supposed to turn back to Hank, but I wasn't ready. "How are you?" I asked, looking her up and down. That was when I noticed her slippers, their little embossed bears staring me cheekily in the face. Where I came from, women wore sneakers for the commute and pumps for the office. In Tokyo they wore heels for the folks on the subway and slippers for the boss. No wonder the men went crazy. These women looked ready for bed at all hours.

"Fine, thank you," she answered, and tried once again to turn to Hank.

"Nice shoes," I said.

She giggled, a little confused, but clearly relieved that I was keeping things mundane.

"Do you have different styles, depending on your outfit, or maybe what mood you're in?"

"Cathy," Hank interrupted, "I think Ikeda-san has things to do."

"Oh, sure. You bet. Sorry. Don't let me keep you."

She left. Hank got up to close the door behind her.

"What the hell was that?" he demanded, turning on me like a bull.

"Is Ikeda-san's bra padded?"

"What?"

"It looks like it to me."

He threw up his arms. "How would I know?"

"Give me the keys, Hank."

"No. What's going on?"

I put out a hand.

He reached into his pocket looking extremely confused.

"Thanks," I said when he'd laid the keys on my palm, warm from his heavy thigh. I turned and put a hand on the door.

"Wait," he said.

I stopped and looked back. His face reminded me of the way he behaved when we started dating, when he really wanted to kiss me.

"You look great," he said. "Where'd you get those clothes?"

"Sook Young," I responded flatly.

"They fit you really well."

"You're surprised?" I still had my hand on the door, but I turned my body a bit toward him.

"I thought you said Japanese clothes didn't fit you."

"Sook Young is Korean."

"Oh," Hank said, nodding. "Uh-huh."

He was looking at my breasts, staring at them like a thirteen-year-old. I watched a hard-on point to the space his keys had left, then begin to fill it. I had known in the taxi that I was going to turn him on. I had been on the war path, and I'd scalped the enemy. But now all I could think was, *Next time, remind me to marry a grown-up.*

"Think she'd let you have the shorts?" he said.

I looked down at Sook Young's clothes. My old red shorts reminded me of the volleyball I used to play, and outlet shopping in Maine.

Although Sook Young's clothes flattered me, they carried her physical memories. "I don't want her shorts, Hank," I told him, and left.

Standing on the sidewalk just outside the door to Hank's building, I watched the people go by. It was late morning now, and well turned-out ladies were climbing out of taxis and paying for exorbitantly priced cups of tea in preparation for visiting Prada, Moschino, Issey Miyake, Max Mara. Two young women had painted their faces white with black lines like cracks down their cheeks. One was dressed like a doll in a pinafore and knee socks. She had ribbons in her hair and carried a basket. After a few moments along came a trio of girls in their early twenties who had clearly made their own clothes. The sun glinted off the shiny threads of the vibrant old kimonos they had cut up to fashion a pair of bell-bottomed pants, a dramatically long jacket, and a miniskirt with a bustle. Some of their hair blew around their necks, the rest was piled in stiff mounds and secured by traditional ornaments—spikes of metal topped with dangling butterflies and flowers in that characteristically Japanese combination of delicacy and danger.

Clearly there was a whole lot more room for imagination in my wardrobe. I had options I'd never considered. But I found I didn't care. The adrenalin was draining out of my body, and the morning's excitement was becoming a colorful snapshot I'd paste in my memory album with the caption: *Not me at all*.

Suddenly I missed Miller, with an ache I knew I didn't have to question. I made my way across the wide sidewalk and hailed a cab, asking the driver to take me home. I only said home because I didn't know how to tell him in Japanese to take me to the daycare center. I'd walk from the apartment. No, I'd run. I couldn't wait to see my little boy. He'd be happy to see me, too. When we walked back to the apartment I'd carry him for a little while, and he'd probably pull my hair and say "Giddyup!" Giddyup I would. It wouldn't matter what I was wearing. Miller liked my simple outfits just fine.

Epistemology of the Fern
SARA PENNINGTON

This world is not my home, I'm just a-passing through.
My treasures are laid up somewhere beyond the blue.
                                                            —Baptist Hymn

In the hollows, in the deep geologic ruts
of Appalachia, old
                saints—the bright sunken eyes,

hair the color of dried bones,
the high voices—
                sing an antiphony: *in this world*
but not of it.

        *

Here, floodwaters groan
against clapboards, the stammering roar,
                                        that tympani
under the creaking soprano of planks. *Noise*
of lack, space that wants
space, crack
                in this place between two: this voice
is both other and neither.

        *

And the pre-flooded field? Green. Yes, it must be green
if it must be
anything at all. And so, part of it:
                                the blue that is not
                                blue, the mirage
of color in the sky. The curvilinear layers more

than the particles, the pollen,
the ancient combusted fern. Has it always been
seen this way: the sky? If the wind did not

bruise itself
                against the firmament, would there
ever have been the green that now recedes?

*

And now of the green that is resurging: tendrils roiling

across corrugated rust. The green finger
                            of rebirth
knowing no floodplain.

*

And so I learn:

I am only a blastula
                of knowledge, a speck
dividing on the tip of a stem, a daughter
cell trapped—parents and progeny, bristling, turgid,
part of it all, threading
                    in either direction,
exponentially, and, too: a ball
around which history gathers, a dandelion seed,
rusting wagon wheel. This life is
            larger than
anything I will ever know. And smaller.

I *Love* My Wife!
Ann Darby

The spasm supervening on a wound is fatal.
—Hippocrates

The doctor saw omens everywhere that morning—in the plume of steam trailing behind the locomotive, in the cottonwoods shimmering by the creek, in the red dog silently watching the doctor's carriage drive out Elbart Road. Even the tears the wind brought to the doctor's eyes warned him. So his first sight of the Pine's house—across a cornfield and through the orchard—did not surprise him: it looked abandoned, the front door flung open to wasps and flies and sparrows.

The doctor had visited many a home where death preceded him. He recognized its wake, or believed he did. The houses of the ill were astir, but the houses of the recently dead—though cluttered with the same medicaments, the same vials and bottles and pans, the same piles of sweat-soaked sheets and nightclothes—were still. And as Dr. Peary passed from the back porch to the kitchen, he detected that stillness in the Pine's home.

He *was* surprised to find Jack Pine sitting on the parlor floor, a hatching crate facing him. The boy must have been sorting his rocks, for pieces of quartz were ranked by one knee, isinglass by the other. He wore overalls but no shirt and took no notice of Dr. Peary. Yet when the man asked where everyone was, the boy said without surprise, "I don't know."

"Now, how's that? Didn't your brothers feed you this morning?"

The boy held a piece of rose quartz up to the light. "No, sir."

"What about your father?"

Jack set the quartz gently into the crate. "He didn't feed me either."

The doctor knelt. "I mean, do you know where he is?"

"Upstairs with Mama. I don't think he's ever coming down."

"You don't, do you?"

For the boy's sake, Dr. Peary did not take the stairs two at a time. He walked calmly and entered the room cautiously, noticing the light from the uncovered windows and then the stench from the pile of sheets. He turned toward the ell and saw Alma. She lay on bare ticking, under the coverlet. Her hair was tangled on the pillow, and she seemed to stare quizzically toward the foot of the bed, as if she had a question for Dr. Peary: *why? why?* The pyrexia must have been terrible, he thought, as high as 110. Though he presumed heart failure or a final breath-stopping spasm, reflexively he touched her wrist and placed his palm before her mouth.

The paradox was that Alma seemed calm. Not yet rigid from death, her body was no longer rigid from tetanus. Her lips didn't sneer; her fingers didn't clutch the air; and her feet were not flexed, though her back arched slightly, as if she were trying to levitate—or scratch a hard-to-reach spot. The position thrust her hips up, and Dr. Peary was embarrassed to find the sight of her aroused him. Perhaps that's why he turned away and at last saw John Pine sitting dully in the chair by the bed.

"John?"

The man didn't answer, and in the moment he remained silent, Dr. Peary gathered up the paraphernalia of pain—the brown bottle and the lisle mask—from John's lap and checked his vitals. Never should have let the man have the chloroform, Dr. Peary swore to himself, never will again. Good way to lose a license.

"Doc," John said.

"Well, hello. What damn thing have you done here?"

John gazed at Alma and then at the doctor. "Nothing."

"This is nothing?" Dr. Peary held up the mask and bottle.

"Just trying to sleep."

"Better ways to do that."

"Gave myself funny dreams."

The doctor nodded. John's four-day beard was rimed with salt, his mouth weighted under the eaves of his mustache. "They couldn't have been too funny."

John thought before he answered, and thinking took time.

"They weren't."

"I'm sorry," the doctor had to say. "Looks like Alma passed in the night."

"Did she?" John regarded his wife again.

"Come on, man, stand up." In the small space between the bed and the wall, Dr. Peary helped John to his feet. "Let's go downstairs."

"Not yet," John said, louder than the doctor would have liked. "I don't want to go."

"I know you don't, but you got to."

"Let me stay."

Dr. Peary paused, glanced down at Alma. There was nothing so terrible in the way she looked. Life had withdrawn, that was all. Still, he couldn't let the man remain. He'd sat there long enough, hadn't he? "We'll come back, I promise. We'll come right back."

Dr. Peary's sister, who kept his accounts for him, liked to say, "Your business is with the living. No one pays you to console him." The doctor wished he could agree, for already he could feel a thirst coming on. But he couldn't. Paid or not, he had to console, at least until the neighbors arrived, and if he couldn't console the grieving, he could console himself by setting the living in motion again.

And so the doctor busied himself. He walked John through the parlor and into the kitchen, nodding (as John did not) at Jack, who now sat on the hatching crate, his rock collection packed away. The doctor settled John Pine in a chair and ladled him a cup of water. He rang the Brennermans, who promised to come right over, then stepped outside to look for the boys. Not finding them, he stepped in again and—having smelt the dirty linen on the back porch—left a message with the Trimbles' nearest neighbor: "There's two day's work at the Pine house, if Beatrice wants it."

The Brennermans arrived, and still the doctor had to stay—for Hap couldn't carry Alma down the stairs alone, and it seemed cruel to ask John to help. That meant the doctor had to wait until Ida Brennerman and her sister Althea were done tending the body. Choosing to leave Hap and John alone in the kitchen, Dr. Peary retreated to the back parlor, where he thought he might sit by himself some minutes, but there he found the Pine's good dining table—where Alma's body would have to rest—covered with catalogues and ledgers and stacks of *Wallace's Farmer*. He cleared the table, then pushed aside the curtain and stepped into the front parlor, meaning to busy himself with a smoke. Yet the boy Jack hadn't carried his rocks upstairs. He remained in the room, standing on his crate and reaching for the mantel clock. Though it wasn't yet ten, the clock read 3:43, its ornate arms open wide.

Jack, who'd been studying the clock face, turned toward the doctor. "It stopped."

"Yes, it did." Dr. Peary wanted to laugh: he should have known right off why the house was so quiet: no damn ticking clock. "But we can fix that, child." He slipped the key out from under the base, gave the works three good twists, then stepped away to fill his pipe with tobacco.

"No, you can't," the boy said after a moment. "It stop stopped."

"That so?" The doctor canted his head and gave the works another good twist and, when the hands still didn't budge, said, "Guess it has."

"Clocks don't die," the boy declared.

"No, they don't," Dr. Peary said. "That man Rubin, I bet he can fix it."

"Some things can't be fixed, can they?"

"Some things," the doctor said, uneasily, "but most can."

"How do you fix a clock?"

"Way you fix most anything. Open it up and see what's wrong inside." Ruing his answer, the doctor tried to divert the boy. "You want me to take the crate upstairs for you?"

"No."

"How about a game of checkers then?"

Jack turned around on his upended crate and said, "Mama died last night."

"Yes, she did," the doctor said. "I'm sorry."

Jack's brow rumpled. "Who's going to make us breakfast? Daniel can't hardly cook at all."

"I suppose he can't."

"Think Mrs. Brennerman will take care of us?"

The boy's overalls were dirty at the knees, and his bare shoulders seemed both knobby and tender.

"Someone will," the doctor said. "Someone will."

By the time the doctor helped Hap roll Alma onto the camp blanket and carry her down to the back parlor, she looked nothing like herself: her hair was tied in a blue ribbon, her cheeks and lips rouged (Althea's doing), her eyebrows greased with Vaseline (also Althea's doing). If John Pine objected, he didn't say. He pressed himself up and followed Alma into the back parlor, watching silently as Hap and the doctor laid his wife on the table and slid the army blanket out from under.

He dug in his pockets and said, "I have no pennies. Will nickels do?"

Hap nodded, and John gave him two, then left the room and

lowered himself like a cripple into his Morris chair. The Brennermans traded wary glances, at last turning to Dr. Peary and casting him a look he recognized from his years in practice: *you're the doctor; you take care of it.*

"No medicine for his troubles," he said. Still, they silently begged him to do *some*thing, so he walked over and leaned close, offering John a sleeping powder for the night.

"I don't need any damn potions."

If John didn't, the doctor did. He'd long ago begun thinking he'd pick up a powder or two at Pogue's. (Surely that woman who suffered the hard birth needed something to ease her pain.) And while Ben Pogue ground the compounds in the back, the doctor would help himself to the bottle of whiskey Ben kept under the counter.

"Suit yourself," the doctor said, then grabbed his bag and jacket from the peg under the stairs. What more could he do? The less he had to do, the stronger his thirst. He stepped into the back parlor to take his leave of the Brennermans. Althea and Hap had taken posts by the body, but Ida stood with her notions—her scissors, needle, and thread, Althea's tins of rouge and Vaseline, the ribbons Ida had collected over the years—gathered in her apron. "You wouldn't mind if I rode with you?" she asked.

"Not at all," the doctor said, though in truth he did: the Brennerman farm was out of his way and keeping him from his drink.

"I'm grateful. Althea's staying, and Hap too, lest John become unruly, but I got to go before my children burn house and barn to the ground."

"That's fine, Ida," the doctor said, and to show he meant it, grasped her elbow. He nodded to Althea, her own head nodded in prayer, and then to Hap, who sat cross-armed, chief of the gallon can of formaldehyde between his feet. (Wise of Hap to bring his own preservative. Somebody had to keep Alma's face from turning purple before they buried her.) The doctor managed one last glance at Alma, which reminded him to say: "You'll want some ice in here, Hap."

"Ice?" Hap said. "Lucky the man's still got some, ain't he?"

Hap wanted to shout to the boys he reckoned were somewhere in shouting range, "We need ice in here." But he couldn't shout in front of the doctor, and once the doctor had driven Ida away, he found he couldn't shout in front of the dead, either. So Hap offered his pardon to

Althea and headed for the front porch. As good a place as any to look for the boys, he figured, though he couldn't really say where he'd last seen them. He hadn't given them a thought. No one had, not even John, who sat in his Morris chair, eyes closed. Hap gazed from the porch toward the orchard, the apple and peach trees, the few cherry trees he coveted, and then east toward the windmill, the brooder and chicken houses, the hog yard and oat bin. The boys'd be in the barn, if they weren't lost in the cornfields, so Hap figured. But as he climbed down the front steps, he heard a small limb crack, and dead ahead young Daniel dropped from the leafy arms of a peach tree, followed by young Will. Hap went straight for the boys and they straight for him, meeting halfway between the orchard and the house.

"Dan! Will!" Hap said, offering a sharp nod to each, then paused, not knowing what the boys knew nor where to begin. "So where've you two been?"

The boys wore hats against the sun, and in their shade, he couldn't see the look passing between them. Daniel said, "We been doing our chores," and Will added, "Then we climbed some trees."

Hap nodded and tried to tug his hat, forgetting he'd forgotten the damned thing. He rubbed his head instead, pondering how the boys could be so ignorant of the goings-on in their house. Hard to imagine them climbing trees when the doctor and the Brennermans themselves were coming and going. But the boys were *just* boys, dusty, barefoot boys, working and loafing and pranking like boys. So Hap said, "Dr. Peary talk to you?"

"No, sir," Daniel said.

"He didn't, eh?" Hap braced himself (damned doctor), then blurted, "I am so sorry about your mother."

Both boys stared at him, but Will said, "She's going to get better, isn't she?" causing Daniel to turn and gawp.

"Oh, brother." Hap wished he could slap his hat across his knee a time or two. "Boys. I got to tell you, your mother died." The boys neither cried nor spoke, though Hap was certain their eyes filled. "I'm so sorry. She's a good woman. Or she was. Uncommonly good."

And still the boys stood dumb as damned immigrants, and Hap didn't know what to do. Daniel at last said, "Thank you, sir," and Will nodded.

And a good thing, too, for Hap had begun to think they'd gone daft. He gazed past the boys, to the inviting shade of the orchard, and remembered why he'd come searching. "I'm sorry to ask, boys, but we need some ice."

"Ice?" Daniel said.

"For the back parlor, where your mother lies."

"To keep her cold," Will asked, "like a carcass?"

"Yes, to keep . . ."

Hap thought better of saying more, but it didn't matter, for what he feared had already happened. Will was crying—not whining or moaning or wailing but weeping silently, tears streaming down his face. Hap shook his head and ran a hand through his thinning hair. Why did he have this terrible job, telling the boy he'd lost his mother?

"I'm sorry, I'm so sorry." Hap clapped his arms around Will, but he may as well have slapped him, for the boy began to sob, big gasping sobs that Hap could do nothing but watch the way, from the shadow of his porch, he could watch lightning cross the countryside. Once the squall passed, Hap handed Will his handkerchief, then dug into his pocket for peppermints or licorice or horehound. (Candy had been known to pacify Hap's children.) When he found nothing but a cigar stub and two bits, he gave the boy the coin, and Will accepted it as if it were nothing more than an acorn or a button.

"I'll get you some ice then," Daniel said.

Hap had all but forgotten the older boy. "You'll want to bring three or four blocks, boy."

"Yes, sir," Daniel said, and set off for the icehouse.

Hap laid a hand on Will's shoulder and guided him past the rose bushes, up onto the porch, and through the parlor where John Pine still sat in his Morris chair, eyes closed and mouth agape. Hap settled the boy at the kitchen table and, needing to do something for him, set out a plate of crackers and preserves. He waited until Will took a bite (had Hap done enough? could he possibly?), then patted the boy's head, pushed aside the damask curtain, and resumed his place beside the body.

Daniel hauled four fifty-pound blocks from the icehouse, one at a time, setting each on the porch. Ignoring his brother, who sat at the table pushing Hap's quarter around with one finger, Daniel hoisted a block to the back parlor, rapping on the jamb before he entered. He looked first at Hap and Althea sitting against the near wall and then across at

118

the open window, where a breeze played with the white curtains. Only then dared he eye his mother.

"Yah," said Hap, "that's exactly what we need here."

Daniel said nothing. His mother was dressed in her best waist and skirt, her good shoes laced on. Her head was tipped forward, as if supported by an invisible pillow, but a rag steeped in formaldehyde covered her face.

"I guess we need a crate or something to set that ice on," Hap said. "Althea! Why don't you root around and find the boy a crate or two for the ice."

"That's all right, Mr. Brennerman. I can find one."

Still hoisting the ice, Daniel grabbed an egg crate from the porch and brought it into the back parlor, where he set down his load. Althea opened the chest, searching for linens or towels to catch the drip, while Daniel rounded up two more crates from the cellar and used the kitchen step stool for the fourth block.

"Maybe we ought to close the window now," Hap said. "Keep the room cooler."

Althea rose to shut the window, but Daniel stammered out, "Excuse me," and she stopped, as if it would be rude to move when a man, or even a boy, spoke. "I believe I'll bring my brothers in here."

"Well, I don't know." Hap rubbed his head, once and then again. "What do you think, Althea?"

"You know I don't know a thing about raising boys."

"This isn't exactly a matter of raising them."

"Near enough," Althea said, and stitched her lips together.

Hap turned toward the boy. "Maybe you should ask your father."

"He said we could."

"What do you mean?"

"He said we could come see our mother." Daniel lied and didn't care.

"Well, I don't think it's right," Althea said, and smacked the window shut.

Which cinched it for Hap. "Aw, go on. Go fetch your brothers," he said, leaving Althea to stare her reproof into the floor.

Here is the truth. At dawn, Will woke Daniel, whispering. *Ma's getting better.* Daniel rolled onto his back and called his brother a liar.

"Am *not*," Will said, and to prove he wasn't led Daniel up the stairs and into the room where their mother lay. "Look!" Will pointed to the bared windows that meant their mother could endure light again. "Look!" He gestured toward the bed. Daniel did look, and the instant he saw her—her skin gray, her mouth rigid in a bitter grin—he understood. Of course the windows were bare. Of course his mother could suffer the light. Daniel would have struck his brother, but Will's knees buckled as if he'd already been struck.

"Boys?"

From a chair crowded in the corner, their father peered at them. His eyes for once were not glinting and inscrutable but wide as ponds and dark as sorrow. And yet, as if everything were ordinary, Father pulled the coverlet up to Mother's chin, saying, "Don't worry, boys. We're fine. I'm fine, your mother's fine. Just . . . a long night. It's morning, isn't it? Haven't you got chores to do?"

They did. They went from the barn to the hog yard to the chicken house, until no chores were left to do. Though they could never explain why, not to their own satisfaction anyway, they couldn't return to the house, so they walked a detour through the cornfield behind the orchard and took lookout posts in the branches of the trees, sometimes sitting, sometimes lying, sometimes climbing higher or lower or moving to another tree. They'd seen the doctor come and go and changed their perches a handful of times, when Will said, "Ma didn't look like that before."

"I know," said Daniel, and those two admissions became a pact between them. And then Mr. B stepped onto the front porch and scanned the out-buildings, and trading a glance, the boys dropped into the grass and walked, hat brims lowered, across the open yard toward Mr. B.

"What'll we say?" Daniel asked.

"Think I know?" Will said.

In the kitchen, Will spun Hap's quarter on the table and Daniel weighed what to say. His brother was pale from crying, and their mother would have given him hot milk with molasses. But Daniel wasn't his mother. He asked, "You done crying?"

"I don't know," Will said. "Ma never died before."

Daniel laughed, despite himself. "You son of a weasel."

"*You* want the quarter?" Will slid the coin toward his brother.

"Course not," Daniel said.

"Neither do I," Will said, and let the quarter gleam on the table. "Does she look different now?"

"She's dressed nice," Daniel said, "but her face is covered." Will hid his face in his arms, so Daniel added, "Mr. Brennerman said we could see her."

"I don't think I want to," Will said.

"I had to ask special," Daniel said. "I had to lie."

"So?" Will said, and lifted his head. "So what?"

"What about Jack? Think he knows?"

Will said, "He doesn't, then you got to tell him."

"I can't."

"I'll give you the quarter if you do."

"I don't want the damn quarter."

Saying no more, they rose together and walked to Jack's small room, Daniel barely minding when Will pocketed the coin. Upstairs, they found their brother kneeling, Mother's mantel clock before him, the back pried open, gears and bolts and coils spread across the pine planks, like an ancient alphabet spilled onto the floor. Jack lifted his face, his hair sifting across his brow, and said, "It stopped."

"Of course it stopped," Daniel said. "No one wound it. What did you think it would do?"

"You're wrong," Jack said. "I wound it." He held up the key for his brothers to see. "The doctor wound it. But it still didn't tick."

Daniel and Will stared at the jumble they believed could never be reassembled—a large hoop and tiny, spoked wheels; a flat disk with miniscule continents carved from it; curved hooks, and screws that ranged from teensy to tiny—and then at each other. The clock had been a wedding present to their parents, as they'd heard many times, and now the present lay in ruins.

"We've got to go downstairs," Daniel said.

"Why?" Jack asked.

Daniel glanced toward Will, who said, "Because Ma died."

"I know," Jack said. "But why've we got to go downstairs?"

"Because," Daniel said, "maybe we won't get another chance to see her."

In the back parlor, the window remained shut, and the damask curtains that served for the back parlor door had been pulled to. Althea and Hap sat with their heads bowed. The room was dimmer now and cooler than before, and the smell of formaldehyde—far worse than the smell of chloroform—sidled into the boys' heads and seeped into their clothes. The boys waited expectantly, yet their mother kept still, her arms taut, her hands cupped as if she meant to scoop bathwater over their heads—a stillness that changed her more than the cloth or the smell or the odd cant of her neck and hips.

Hap coughed, to suggest the boys leave, but Will took it as his cue to break rank and lift the rag from his mother's face, which he did before Daniel could stop him. As quickly as he lifted it, Will dropped it to the floor. He reached to lift the nickels that mocked his mother's gray eyes, but Hap said, "Son," and Will took her hand instead. It was cool but not limp (it was beginning to stiffen), and sure her hand was squeezing his, he began to weep again. A long moment he held the pose of a son saying farewell, the tears his brothers could not cry guttering down his face. Then Hap thought to cough again, and Will stepped back.

Daniel eyed his brother askance, then picked up the rag and re-covered his mother's face. Jack said, "Ma's hair looks real nice."

Althea said, "Doesn't it?"

That night, Hap and Althea took turns sitting up with Alma. Truth be told, it was Althea who remained awake most of the night. It was awkward, because all night John Pine remained in the front parlor, sitting in his Morris chair, which was where Hap, for one, wanted to sleep, and Althea, too, not that she admitted it. Instead, they slept in the kitchen, on those hard wooden chairs. A damned uncomfortable way to sleep, Hap later told Ida.

First light, John rose and walked through the kitchen and out the back door on his way to the privy. Poor Hap, he thought. Just look at him sprawled on the kitchen table. Returning, John put a hand on Hap's back, murmuring, "Good man, good man." Then he pushed open the curtain to the back parlor. (He remembered Alma ordering that damask. "Just tablecloth goods," she said, "but it'll make nice curtains, don't you think?"). He saw that his wife still lay where he'd left her, and then he took in the rest of the room, the white curtains Alma had made, trimmed with lace she'd tatted. Her Chicago writing machine standing on its small desk, and crowded next to it, the Singer he bought her before the first baby, the mending piled atop it. It struck him odd at first, the four bricks of ice sitting atop three crates and a kitchen stepstool crowded around the table. Then he saw the soaked towels and linens beneath them. (Even the crumb cloth was drenched.) And he remembered who had died; he understood the need for ice.

Althea looked at him from the straight-back chair where she had sat most the night, a coal-oil lamp casting a greasy light on the prayer book in her hands, and said very quietly, "Good morning, John."

"Morning, Althea."

He gazed again at Alma, then pulled the curtain shut behind him and went down to the icehouse he was so proud to build last year, with its cement walls and its tidy drains—an icehouse so thick, so impervious to sun and rain it would keep the ice harvest until the first snow—returning with a block of ice, which he set on the back parlor floor. He went down again and returned with another block he set next to the first. After his third trip, Althea said, "John?"

"Althea?" he said, and headed back to the icehouse.

"What are you doing, man?" Hap asked.

Hap woke slowly, his back achey, his mind scarcely turning, but he was alert enough to watch his neighbor bring three blocks of ice through the kitchen and into the back parlor. The fourth provoked the question. "Did the ice melt down?"

"Near to," John said before heading out again.

"Well, I guess it might have. It was a hot night."

Hap pushed himself up from the table, dimly thinking that his wife would drop by to fix breakfast and wouldn't that be nice after this long night? He went to the back parlor to say good morning to his sister-in-law and saw not the four blocks he expected to see but blocks and blocks of ice set on the floor and stacked atop each other, a low but growing wall.

"What in God's ..."

"*Hap*," Althea said.

"Well, you'd curse, too, Althea," he said, then added, "why *aren't* you cursing?"

"What good would that do?"

"You've been watching him do this?"

"Well, I'm not blind. Not last time I looked."

"How long's he been at this?" Hap asked.

"Long enough for you to wake up and notice."

"Why didn't you stop him?"

"And how am I supposed to do that?"

John pushed back the curtain, another block of ice on his shoulder, and Hap asked again, "What are you doing?"

"Bringing up the ice."

"All of it?"

"If that's what it takes."

"You could have told the doctor and me. We would have put Alma in the cellar."

"I don't want my wife in the cellar. What do you think? She's a potato sprouting from its eyes?"

John shouted this into Hap Brennerman's face loud enough the boys lying in their beds heard it, loud enough the dogs sleeping under the porch and the chickens scratching in the yard heard it. Then John swung the ice down, a bit too close to Hap's face, and set the block near Alma's feet.

"I'm just being practical, John. You don't have ice, you won't be able to keep butter."

"No reason to *keep* butter if there's no one to make it."

"All right, all right," Hap said, and sat down next to Althea. "I won't argue that. But let me ask, why are you doing this? You want to wait a couple days for Alma's sister to get here? You want to bring your mother down from Abilene?"

"Why would I wait for *them*?"

John let the door slap behind him, but when he returned, this time precariously carrying a block on each shoulder, he said, "I just want to keep her, Hap. That's all. I just want to keep her."

So John did. He kept his wife as long as he could. Hap and Althea had to excuse themselves: they couldn't hold but one night of this vigil. Hap had his wife and children to consider, Althea had her sister, and they both had the farm to worry about. They'd be pulling corn soon, and hadn't John better be thinking about that himself? Althea did offer to cook meals twice a day. The children had to be fed, after all. But John said, no, *he* would take care of Alma and the boys, *they* would take care of the stock, and the crops would have to wait, even if the corn wasn't pulled and the wheat not sown. And who cared what they ate, anyway?

Hap and Althea drove away in the wagon, while John continued bringing ice from the icehouse. ("Must have been a ton of it," Hap Brennerman told the men at Ward's.) John closed up the Singer and removed the Chicago writing machine from its desk, setting blocks on top of them. He hoisted ice atop the linen chest and onto the corner piece where Alma stored her mother's dishes. As best he could, he filled the room with ice, even padding blocks in old sheets and placing them gently next to his wife.

Despite the protests of his neighbors, despite the counsel of his pastor, despite the stories he knew were told in town, John and the boys accepted no visitors all the days the ice melted and soaked through everything—warping the corner piece and the linen chest and the sewing machine cabinet and the writing desk, warping the very table on which Alma lay. They lived in isolation, but for the Trimble girl—who, after getting word from her nearest neighbor, set up a washtub on the far side of the barn (where John Pine wouldn't see her) so she could tend to the reeking bedclothes someone had tossed into the yard. And they lived in silence, but for the sound of water dripping—from the table or desk or cabinet to the sodden floorboards, from the sodden floorboards to the stone cellar below. All those days, John Pine forbade his boys to answer the door when Ida Brennerman knocked or the pastor stood in the yard shouting, "Anybody home?"

John made only one trip to town. Having used up Hap's formaldehyde, John went to Ward's to buy a gallon, so he'd be sure to have a fresh rag every hour for Alma's face. That's when the rumor started that John Pine shared this duty with his boys. That he asked them to dip and wring the rags and spread them over their dead mother's face.

It must have taken ten days for the ice to melt. Date of death and date of burial—those are recorded. Though she died September 8th, Alma May Pine was buried in the Promise Township cemetery September 19th, 1913. As grown men, the boys claimed they remembered none of this. Only Jack allowed as how he might. "And, really, I'm probably remembering what I was told over the years. And what medical school taught me. She was beginning to bloat, you know. But we couldn't see that, because of her clothing. Father lifted her as gently as you'd lift a sleeping child and laid her in that casket he'd built. The town had by then a lacquered black wagon with glass windows and brass lamps, and she was carried in that hearse to the Promise cemetery and laid to rest in an improper service. Father paid his plot fee all right, and he paid the carting fee for the hearse, but no pastor presided, no relative was invited. Just us, standing under those elm trees long since deceased."

Early Morning at the Petting Zoo
MIKE WHITE

Maintenance is out
smoking in brown coveralls,
dragging shovels.

In the shadow
of the ferris wheel,
bright hints of deer.

Iceland
MIKE WHITE

It always felt as though our house was someplace
Colder than it should have been. But I was a child;
Encircling sea and island home were all my
Life and dreams. Dad built a ship in my sleep.
Alone he sailed to find warm harbors where
No one spoke a language he would miss;
Dark water all around, no sail between the sea and sky.

North to Alaska in the Sixties
BURNS ELLISON

North to Alaska!
Go north, the rush is on
North to Alaska!
Go north, the rush is on!
—Johnny Horton

We remained all morning in bed. In the afternoon I walked with her to her class. I didn't know what to say so I talked about Ireland. I was off to Alaska, but what I talked about was what we had once planned to do together—go to Ireland and live in a cabin in the "bee-loud glade." We'd spend the days delving into the Celtic past, poking through musty archives in old libraries, reading myths and folk tales, seeking out evidences of the "little people." And we'd visit Yeats' grave, and fish for salmon in the Irish streams and take walks through the heather, and at night I would comb her long hair. And we'd have thick warm quilts and a big wide bed, and pots of tea to drink by a sputtering fire, while outside the banshee winds shrieked, the rains poured down, and the mists moved in from the sea. Weekends we'd go to the village pub and drink with the locals, and on June 16th we'd be off to Dublin to celebrate Bloomsday. And I wanted so badly to believe what I was saying, and that I could still make it all come true.

I held her, not wanting to let her go, not wanting to leave her. I kissed her, and told her that I loved her. Her eyes were moist and glistening, but then so were mine, along with everybody else's. The day before, helicopters had tear-gassed the campus and sheriff's deputies had stood on the roof of the student union lobbing canisters on the demonstrators below, and our eyes still burned from the fumes.

In downtown Berkeley the police were making mass arrests, hauling protesters off in busloads. Helicopters circled overhead. There were smashed store windows, the sidewalks covered with broken glass, here and there stains of blood. I passed a firstaid station where some scraggly bearded young kid was getting his head bandaged. I stood on the corner waiting for the light to change. Two cops seized the guy next to me and dragged him away. Another cop ordered me to keep moving.

On University Avenue I took my turn behind the lines of hippies with packs and rolls and taped-together suitcases, waving signs and placards that said: New York and Chicago, Denver, Taos, and Los Angeles. A couple of women carried babies. All of them could have been gypsies or Bedouins, exotic refugees fleeing from a city besieged. The day was sunny and hot, which only made the fumes of tear gas burn more.

Early afternoon: a street corner in Blaine, Washington. Wondering how I was going to get past the Canadian customs, I noticed the Volkswagen with California plates parked across the street. Glistening black, glittering with chrome, mammoth ballooning tires. With the driver standing next to it. He wore a black Stetson cowboy hat, black shades, black Levi's, and a black parka with a Laguna Seca patch on the shoulder and an American flag on the breast. He had black sideburns, and a black goatee, and he was just then lighting himself a cigarette.

…Luis Garcia Mendoza was his name, and he was from Lima, Peru, by way of Monterey, California, and I found this out while we sat in a café drinking coffee, and yes, he, too, was on his way to Alaska. But "these bastards at the customs"—they would not let him through. And he had not slept since leaving Monterey, and he had been driving very hard, and now "these—these sons-of-bitches"—they would not let him through because of insufficient funds, even though his billfold—he shook it at me—bulged with credit cards. Yes, he would take me across the border, but even if we pooled funds—mine being what they were— we'd still be turned back.

We went outside and sat on the curb. A cop pulled up in his cruiser, asked to see our IDs, then ordered us off the curb. We went back inside the café and drank more coffee. The shadows of late afternoon lengthened, and the cop was still cruising back and forth, keeping an eye on us. I was wondering about trying to cross the border on foot when Luis got up saying he was going to call his mistress in Monterey and ask her to wire him money. Twenty minutes later, he was back. He sat down, cursing. His mistress wasn't home, so he'd called her mother for money and she had turned him down. He sat there, biting his lip, rapping his spoon on the counter. Then he was back on his feet. There was no help-ing it—he would call his wife.

Afterward, we drove to the closest Western Union, in Bellingham. While waiting for his money order to arrive, we shaved and showered at a YMCA. Once he had his money, Luis insisted we have dinner at a nearby steakhouse, where he told me more about himself. A piano player by vocation and sports car racer by avocation, he was on his way to Anchorage, Alaska to make his fortune so he could then one day go back to Peru and hold his head high, prove to people he wasn't just his father's wastrel playboy son.

After we'd had dinner, we breezed through customs, and then a few miles up the road in Canada I asked him if he'd drop me off at the next gas station.

"No way, Eduardo," he said. "*Mi amigo*—my friend. You are going to Alaska. I am going to Alaska. We are going to Alaska. I could not leave you behind. This country is full of wild animals, perhaps bandi-tos. I would worry for you."

"But Luis," I said. He had no room. He had removed his backseat and crammed the rear to the roof with spare tires, spare parts, a five-gallon can of gas, cans of oil, clothes, bags, and suitcases. He'd packed more spare tires under the hood, no room for anything there. Backpack and sleeping bag on my lap, knees jammed against the glove compart-ment, I could hardly move. If I turned my head one way, there was his machete in its bejeweled leather scabbard; if I turned the other, I found myself looking down the barrel of his .22.

"No sweat. We will make room. Play some music." Luis had tapes of the pianist Floyd Cramer with him. Floyd Cramer was his idol. So I played Floyd Cramer while Luis drove through the verdant coastal countryside, through towns just coming to life on a Saturday night. Then we were going through the city of Vancouver, and though I couldn't tell for sure, it seemed to me that we were going the wrong way.

Dusk, driving through a lush green park. Groves of tall conifers, ter-raced, spacious green lawns and rolling green hills. Beds of flowers and ponds with ducks and swans. All so very idyllic—except that every-thing was too much a blurred succession of images passed before me on a speeded-up roll of film. Only I wasn't comfortably seated in some dark movie theater with my box of popcorn. I had the sense of being on a roller coaster, careening around curves—loops and twists of highway unraveling before us. Cars and trucks whizzed by, tires screeched, horns blared. I glimpsed signs, but trying to read them left me with my stomach in my mouth. Then—finally—a stop sign, and a brief respite. And there a cop appeared. On his motorcycle. A mechanized Royal Canadian Mountie, no less. Well, maybe not a Mountie, but nonetheless a cop—and he'd pulled up to us, and we'd been waved over.

Luis got out of his car and walked back to him, produced his identification. They talked, and went on talking. Meantime, nothing I could do but sit and wait. Finally, Luis came back to his car—grinning. It seemed the Mountie himself was owner of a souped-up Volkswagen, and they had been comparing vehicles. Much relieved, I was also annoyed—because of course all this time I'd been worrying that we were about to be thrown in jail or escorted back to the border. Then I remembered wondering if we were going the right way. Luis checked back with the Mountie, and yes, it seemed we'd gotten turned around. But *no problema*—he would make up for lost time. The Mountie gave us a cheery smile as we drove by. He had round pink cheeks, looked cherubic; and my heart went out to him.

The road leveled out, and, strapped into my seat belt, my pack between me and the windshield, I began to relax while Floyd Cramer played on the tape deck and Luis talked about his car. Those mammoth-ballooning tires: brand new four-ply racing tires, they were. And the engine: souped-up to go over ninety miles an hour. And that steering wheel: teak? mahogany? It was hand-carved, exuded an oily fragrance. When I reached over to touch it, Luis blocked my hand. The wheel was hair trigger, the least nudge, and we could go flipping end over end.

Luis had spent hours on his car, and thousands of dollars. He nursed and cherished his car like a baby. All the improvements and embellishments, all the fine tuning done on the engine, he had done himself. He would not let anyone else touch his car. The idea of somebody else lifting up the hood and tinkering with a carburetor or gasket was as unthinkable as the idea of somebody else lifting up his wife's skirt. Luis loved his car, knew its every part, was responsive to its every sound, quirk, and mood. Luis and his car were one.

Abruptly, Luis asked me what I could tell him about the "poossee" of the north.

"The what?"

"The poossee! You know, the girls—ah, and you must also tell me, do the ski-moose works spells?"

"The what? Who?"

"The ski-moose! You know, how do you say—the indijenos."

"Oh, you mean Eskimos. I thought you were talking about moose."

"Moose?"

"Yes, the animal. You know, it's like a ... caribou—"

"The what? The car-uh-boo?"

"Yeah, like a deer! The animal with antlers, horns—"

"Oh—deer! Like Roo-dolph! Ah, *comprendo*, I understand."

"And ski-moose working spells, eh?" I started to laugh, but Luis informed me that was not to be taken lightly. Two of his friends traveling through Peru had once stopped at an inn for the night. At the inn were two maids, both of them fat and ugly. His two friends were both handsome and rich. Yet they both fell madly in love with the two maids and married them! And why? Because the two maids had worked spells on them! They had concocted a potion, possibly something with a woman's menstrual flow in it, perhaps the blood of a serpent. When his friends had dinner, drops of the potion were added to their coffee. "Just drops—that was all it took!"

It was dark now, the road once more pitching and winding—and hemmed in by trees, once more I felt like I was on a rollercoaster, with no visibility at all except for the fleeting shafts of the headlights. And rounding each curve I had horrific visions of encountering a moose there before us, frozen in the headlights' glare, and Luis with no time to stop and nowhere to turn.

On the outskirts of a small mountain town, we stopped at a café for coffee. Luis wanted to keep driving, but when I got out of the car I could hardly walk for having been so scrunched in and knotted up, and all I wanted was to stop for the night.

The café was empty except for a large, dumpy-looking waitress sitting behind the counter who didn't even look up when we walked in and sat down. She thumbed through a magazine, picking her nose, while we just sat there—and I was afraid Luis was going to get up and leave.

"Ma'am, could we maybe get some service?"

Grudgingly, heaving a sigh, she waddled over to our table.

"Luis, get yourself a hamburger," I urged.

"No," the waitress said grumpily, "the grill is closed."

"All right, we'll have coffee and pie," I said quickly. After she'd come back with our orders, I suggested we stop for the night. But no, he wasn't tired.

"But Luis," I said, "think of all the scenic vistas you'll be missing, and all the pictures you won't be able to take. Look, you could send snaps to your wife and mistress in California—and more snaps to your family in Peru. Luis, you might never have such a chance again. And, hey, I'll take care of the motel. After all, where would I be if it wasn't for you."

"All right, my friend, if that is what you wish."

I sat back in my chair, immensely relieved. Luis had his cup of coffee to his mouth.

"Luis . . ." He looked at me, puzzled. I nodded at his cup, then glanced meaningfully at the waitress, who'd gone back to her magazine and picking her nose—and the next thing he'd spewed coffee all over the table and we were both giggling away like schoolboys.

Later we found ourselves walking on a footbridge in the cold moonlight over a silver-gleaming creek to a small log cabin tucked away in the woods. But the cabin only had one double bed.

"Luis, let me go get my sleeping bag. You're the one doing all the driving—I'll sleep on the floor."

"What? I will not hear of such a thing. My friend, the bed is big enough for both of us."

During the night I woke up, a bare arm draped over my shoulder. I tried to pull away, but I was already pushed to the edge of the bed. I lay there, thinking of Melville's Ishmael waking up to find himself in the arms of Queequeg, the wild man harpooner from the South Seas. And here I was, in the arms of this rifle-toting, machete-wielding wild man from Peru. I thought about nudging him, asking him to move over. He mumbled something—was he awake? No, he was snoring away, sleeping soundly. Dreaming perhaps of his wife or mistress—or perhaps of "poosee" in general. Finally I went back to sleep, wishing it was Lu-eeze rather than Lu-eese lying next to me.

A glorious morning, green and shining. And such a stirring in the small mountain towns of British Columbia. Information booths with tourist maps, free coffee, and doughnuts. And smoking sawmills and acres and acres of freshly cut timber. And trucks everywhere. We stopped at a filling station where the attendant complained that for good fishing anymore he had to go to Colorado.

And Luis now wanted snaps of himself with the "scenic vistas." We stopped, and click, click—I took them. Then we were off and descending upon the car ahead as though we were going to drive it off the road. We were almost upon it, I braced myself, and then at the last possible split second, Luis touched that hair-trigger steering wheel, and WHOOSH! We had shot past it and were snaking around some hairpin canyon curve, a craggy gorge gaping below, a rumbling, thundering lumber truck ripping by from the other way. I had my sleeping bag billowed in front of me—WHOOSH! WHOOSH! Briefly we'd stop—click, click. Then we were off again—WHOOSH! WHOOSH!

By midday the pace began to tell. Floyd Cramer was wearing thin on the tape deck, there were squalls of rain, and there was the matter of the guns. Along with the rifle in the rear, Luis had a .357 Magnum revolver stowed under the seat. At a roadside café he brought it out, set up a couple of cans on a fence post, and started blasting away. The owner of the café came charging out.

"What the hell are you doing? There's people all around here, I've got pets and livestock! There's no telling what a stray bullet might hit!"

"What kind of country ees thees that I cannot shoot my guns?" Luis cried indignantly. "Who do you think you are, telling me what I cannot do?"

Mumbling apologies to the guy, I got Luis back to his car.

"Luis, goddamnit, you've got to keep your guns out of sight—we could get in real trouble."

"Okay, okay," he said, "but if I see a moose or a car-uh-boo, I am going to shoot it!"

Once back on the road we began encountering more potholes. But instead of slowing down Luis only drove faster. He dodged some of the potholes, others he flew right over. And others he hit jarringly, cursing with every bone-shaking, car-shuddering jolt. Best as I could—between jolts and thuds—I began reading aloud to Luis from one of the travel brochures I'd picked up about the pleasures of taking the Inland Passage, of riding on the ferry from Prince Rupert, British Columbia, to Haines, Alaska. The brochure described floating past fiords and bays and islands, the lush northern rainforest rising up from the water's edge. It described leaning over the rails to watch dolphins cavorting in the wake. Ah yes, lounging in the bar and dinners by candlelight, the car in the steerage and the guns stashed safely away—and I realized how much I was dreading the road ahead. Now I knew how nineteenth century sailors must have felt at the prospect of rounding the Horn. The Alaska Highway—

"Yeah, Luis, 1,500 miles long, and twelve hundred of that is gravel. Yeah, 1,200 miles of fucking gravel and rocks and potholes, and when it rains—goddamned mud! Luis, from everything I've ever heard, it's a man-killer! There's markers all along the way that tell you how many people died from going off into canyons or crashing into trees. And, Jesus, what I hear it does to cars—from what they say, the road can just wreck your car! Luis, the road is a monster!"

But I didn't need to go on. Luis was already concerned, his car wasn't sounding right, was making complaints. He hadn't known that this would be such a road, and we hadn't even gotten to the "monster" part of it.

"Yes, Eduardo, we will take the ferry, and perhaps, who knows, we will find poosee aboard."

Unfortunately, in Prince George we found out we'd have to wait three days to get on the ferry, and it would cost too much, anyway. I urged Luis to wire home for more money. As for me, he wouldn't be leaving me in the lurch. Any ride I got now would probably be going straight through.

"No way, my friend. Do you think I would leave you behind? Besides, who would take my pictures with the scenic vistas?"

So on to the North we drove, and into more and more potholes until we were both hearing the distinct sounds of scrapings. We stopped, and discovered that the rear fenders of the car were cutting into the tires. Okay, Luis had brought along smaller, standard-sized spare tires, and he could have put them on, but that would have meant removing his racing tires, and he wasn't about to do that.

So we scraped into the next town. Only to find out that the one local garage was closed for the weekend. Stopping at a filling station, Luis and the attendants conferred. Phone calls were made, somebody named Bill said he'd be down as soon as he finished dinner.

While we were waiting, a pair of local hotrodders in a 1954 two-tone red and white Ford convertible stopped by. Thumbs hooked into the back pockets of their snug, low-slung jeans, they circled around Luis and his car. They were like tall bristly dogs warily sniffing at the stranger's car—I almost expected one of them to lift his leg. Then the ritual observed, they climbed back into their car and, turning on the radio full blast, peeled off into the sunset.

An hour went by. I thumbed through an old newspaper while Luis and the attendants talked car talk, a language as foreign to me as if they had been speaking in Urdu. Finally, Luis got tired of waiting for Bill to show up. The attendants made more phone calls, and a gawky young guy was found who cut the skirts of Luis's fenders off with a blow torch. He was pretty shaky, though, and the fenders wound up as jagged as the teeth of a shark.

Luis drove into a drizzling cold rain, and with every curve I braced myself. It would be instantaneous—the moose before us in a blinding glare of light, outrageously huge, its rack of antlers wide as the road. "Luis, this car wouldn't have a chance! Moose have been known to charge trucks—buses—trains! As for Volkswagens—"

But Luis wasn't impressed. How could "mooses" compare to what he had seen in the jungles of Peru? And roaring through the night and the wilds of British Columbia, the rain turning to sleet, I found myself listening, for all my fears, while Luis told me of the "shu-shoopa," most dreaded snake in all of "la selva." Larger than the anaconda, and "muy peligroso"—more dangerous than the fer-de-lance! And Luis himself, when only a boy, on a trip to the jungle with his father, had seen one attack a native girl bathing in a river. Swimming up behind the girl, the snake had flicked its tail and, like a bullwhip, struck her. Then, gathering her into its coils, it had sunk back in the river.

"Nothing could be done. We were helpless. In its tail there is a duct filled with poison. The shu-shoopa strikes you, and you are dead! Ah, my friend, there is so much more I could tell you. The jungle, it is no place to be, believe me."

My eyes closed, I drifted off, waking to needles of sleet dancing in the headlights. Then I woke up, and we were parked along the side of the road. Snow was piled up on the windshield, and Luis was curled up asleep. I wrapped my sleeping bag around me, but I was too cold to go back to sleep. I began thinking about Louise. Longing for her, wondering when, if ever, I would see her again. All my dithering and vacillating, my comings and goings, only this time going knowing that there might not be any more coming back. Chilled to the bone, I felt lonely and sad, the most wretched of men. I'd wanted to dare all, do something bold, but what I had embarked upon was sheer fucking folly. Wanting to be true to the dreams of mine youth, but what about hers and those we had once shared? She'd said the only flag I could rally around was my own—so was that true? I glanced over at Luis. Him wanting to make good so he could return to Peru and hold his head high. Me wanting to atone for things and prove myself worthy. Him and me, we were one and the same. Peas from the same pod, both of us equally daft, equally deluded. Wanting to dare all—and I knew just then exactly what I should do. I should shake Luis, rouse him up, and demand we turn around and go back—now! Before it was too late for both of us. Instead I sat and watched the night slowly pale to a cold gray dawn, the snow falling softly, silently. And the trees kept their watch, hulking, shaggy and spectral, mute and unmoving.

Once through the town of Dawson Creek, British Columbia, there it began: the Alaska Highway. And no sooner had we left the paved road behind than the snow ceased to fall, the clouds rolled back, and the sun burst through. Such a propitious sign! I looked to Luis—and he was using both hands to light a cigarette with his knee braced against the wheel—and we were on gravel and he was going eighty miles an hour! Next he had his camera out, and click, click—he himself was taking snaps of the "scenic vistas." But no stopping and losing time, he snapped them on the fly. And we were on gravel. Gravel with potholes and ruts, and rocks sharp as coral. I was terrified! Luis—let me light your cigarettes, let me take the snaps!

Then we were barreling up a long grade, closing in on a car with California plates. We were riding on the guy's rear, but he hugged the middle of the road, wouldn't let Luis go by. We were eating clouds of dust, rocks pinging against the windshield—"That son of a bitch! He is throwing stones at me!"

Abreast of the car, wildly fishtailing on the road's soft shoulder—then we'd shot past the car and we were flying over the crest of the grade, Luis slapping my knee, chortling: "Eduardo, my friend, you must learn to relax."

Clutching my sleeping bag, I stared straight ahead. To let my attention wander I knew would be curtains. I could influence things only to the extent that I kept my eyes riveted on the road. I dozed, my head fell forward, then it snapped back, my eyes popped open—we were spinning into space!

"Eduardo, what do you think the record is for driving this road? I should have contacted sports car clubs, talked to my dealer. I might have found a sponsor. Ah, my friend, a world's record for driving this son-of-a-bitching road! Think of the publicity! Think of the poosee!"

Two hundred miles farther, climbing another long grade. Luis had the pedal to the floor, but we'd only barely made it to the top of the grade when the engine died. The tank was half full of gas, yet when he tried to start the car back up—nothing. The engine refused to turn over, not a sound. He pumped the pedal, tried again. Nothing. We got out of the car and he checked the engine. He got back in the car and I got behind it and pushed. It started to roll and I jumped back in. He shifted gears, popped the clutch. The car jumped, then rolled to a stop.

We sat there, on an open ridge, the sun shining, snow melting, the northern spruce forest stretching for as far as I could see in every direction. Luis bit his lips, rapped his knuckles against the steering wheel. Then he jumped out of the car and started unloading it—spare tires, clothes, bags, and suitcases—until he'd found his toolbox. Opening it, he dumped everything out. After finding the tools he was looking for, he peered under the car's hood, tightening this, adjusting that. Then he got back in the car and again tried to start it. Again nothing.

"Goddamn son of a bitch!" He banged his fist on the dashboard.

A car with a British Columbia license pulled up. Luis asked the driver if he had jumper cables. The guy didn't but he said there was a truck stop some thirty miles ahead and that he could drive him there if he wanted to get a tow truck. Luis turned to me.

"Eduardo, I am entrusting you with my car. This is *muy importante*. Can I ask you to do that? Will you be here when I return?"

"Yes, Luis, I will be here on your return," I said, feeling annoyed that he would even need to ask.

After they left, I got out of the car and found a place dry enough to lie down. I wasn't merely resigned to a long wait, I was looking forward to it. It was such a warm and lovely day, everything so peaceful. Faint sounds of birds, bright sun and blue sky overhead, spruce trees all around me, thick and green as grass. A big glossy black raven lit on a nearby stump. I threw a few croaks at it, trying to drum up a conversation. The raven tilted its glossy black head and gave me a quizzical look, but it wasn't croaking.

The sky clouded over. Everything that Luis had taken out of his car—I got up and put it all back as it started to rain. Afterward, I sat in the driver's seat and, having nothing else to do, fiddled around with the steering wheel. Then, just for the hell of it, I turned the key in the ignition—and the car started right up! And there I sat while it purred away, vibrating with all that horsepower just waiting to be unleashed. Quickly, I turned the engine off, not knowing what it might do. But of course I couldn't leave it at that. I tried again, and again, the car started. Then, hesitantly, fearfully, I set forth.

I found Luis in a truck stop café, waiting impatiently for somebody with a tow truck to show up.

"What are you doing here?" he cried when he saw me. "I left you to look after my car!"

I told him I'd driven it here, and that it was parked out in front. He rushed outside to have a look, then came back.

"What did you do?" he wanted to know. "How did you make it start?"

"I just turned the key, that was all—"

"I do not understand this."

"Luis, what can I say? Maybe it's just having a rapport with machines. You know, some people have it with horses, others with dogs."

Luis stepped toward me—I thought he was going to hit me. "My friend, do you know what I think? I think you are, how do you say it?—blowing up my ass with smoke."

Clapping his hands to catch the waitress's attention, he ordered me to sit down. "Whatever you would like, I want for you to have. You have earned it. What's more," he said as he sat down to join me, "after I have set a world's record for driving this road, I will see to it you get credit as my second driver. How does that sound to you?" He grabbed me by the shoulder. "Ah, yes, think Eduardo what that will mean. Such poosee as you have never before known—believe me!"

But after that no more snaps of "scenic vistas," not even on the fly. Luis smashed through potholes and ruts, plowed through sand, gravel, mud, and clay. Flying rocks splintered the windshield and shattered the headlights, there was choking dust everywhere. And now, much as he loved his car, he was being absolutely unsparing of it. He was punishing the car, and himself. And as for the road, he was assaulting it. He would beat it down, humble it, break its spirit, driving his car at seventy-five and eighty miles an hour, at eighty-five and ninety, chain smoking all the while.

"Relax, my friend, relax!" he cried, slapping my knee. "How many times must I tell you!"

Evening: luminous and spring-like—the sky again clear and blue. Hunched to the wheel, jaw clenched, lips thin and bloodless, Luis was now driving along the Coal River, his car churning through a glutinous black bog like a fish across the bottom of a slough. Jets of black ooze splattered the windshield, and rocks, gravel, and mud beat against the floorboards of the car like hordes of subterranean creatures trying to force their way up. We fishtailed from one side of the road to the other—momentarily high-centered, the engine screaming, tires spinning for traction—then abruptly we sprang forward, bouncing and thudding through more potholes and bog.

Suddenly Luis slammed his car to a stop. Cursing, howling with rage, he beat his fists against the steering wheel. His sunglasses started to fall off—he grabbed them and flung them. Then, seizing the steering wheel as though he were about to bite it, he bit his words instead, spit them out: "This motherfucker! It is wrecking my car! This goddamned motherfucking road is destroying it! If I had sticks of dynamite, I would blow this fucking road up! Nobody would ever use it again! You can see, can't you—what it is doing to my car!"

Grabbing his rifle from behind my seat, he lunged out of the car, looking for something to shoot. Birds, rabbits, porcupines—anything. He spun around in the half-light of dusk, within the dense stands of spruce and birch. Briefly, rifle poised, he glared at his car—or was it at me? Then he began firing off round after round into the air, at trees, stumps, boulders—at whatever seemed to offer itself as a target.

I took cover, knees on the floor of the car. The rifle empty—or maybe he had jammed it, Luis took it by the barrel and smashed it against a tree, then whirled about and threw it into the forest. Then he strode back, got back in the car, and sat behind the wheel. I looked over at him. He was crying. Not knowing what to say, I just sat there. Finally I asked if he would like me to drive. He shook his head. We kept sitting there, neither of us saying anything. The trees were massed to the road's edge on both sides; it was as though they had moved in closer, and were leaning over, waiting to see what would happen next.

"All right, my friend, you take it," Luis said. "I do not want to drive now. I am too disgusted."

I got out of the car to go find his rifle. When I came back I found him in the passenger's seat, already asleep.

And now the dusk had given way to night and I was at the wheel of the rollercoaster. Leaving British Columbia, we entered the Yukon Territory. The Yukon—the name alone so magical, so evocative. And this was no mere province. Like Huck Finn, I had lit out for the territory. And I could feel the wilderness all around me, almost palpable, of a different quality from that which we had just left behind. It was of a wildness more remote, more lonely, somewhere out there riding on the winds the Windigo…

I drove slowly, taking the potholes with great care, sometimes coming to almost complete stops as I went over them or around them. But my fears were now gone. I was in a reverie. I reminded myself that this in itself might be cause for concern, but the reminder only vaguely registered. Luis was sleeping. There was only me at the wheel and a-going deeper and deeper into the Yukon. And I was in a lovely warm reverie—yet I was alert, I had my senses about me, I was focused, my powers of concentration never greater. I was one with the car and the road, the trees and the night—Spell of the Yukon, it truly was. And the light running ahead, spearing the darkness, but there was no catching up with it, or outrunning the darkness behind—unless, of course, I speeded up, just a bit. And the road went on and on, only now it was no longer vertiginous and terrifying, it was lulling and dream-like—almost, I could have relinquished the wheel, let my attention lapse, because no matter, I was bound to the road, there was no veering off. The road bore me along like a stream, the car and road an unbroken flow.

And now I was coasting along at fifty and sixty miles an hour, dodging rocks and potholes like a broken-field runner—and OH CHRIST! HOLY SHIT!—I'd gone crashing into a horrendous gaping hole and Luis and I were tossed violently up against the roof of the car. Clutching desperately at the wheel to keep the car on course, I kept driving, pushing and elbowing Luis back to his side of the front seat.

When I stole a glance—he was staring at me, wide-eyed, dazed.

"Luis, no sweat, nothing to worry about—everything's okay," I said. And too exhausted, too out-of-it to respond, Luis went back to sleep, knees tucked, his hands clasping my sleeping bag to his mouth, like an infant in its blanket.

I drove on but much as I wanted to convince myself otherwise, everything was not "okay"—the car was definitely not sounding the same. But I was afraid to stop and see what was wrong. I could only keep going and hope that whatever was wrong would go away. And for a while I succeeded in doing that; at least there were no more sounds of something dragging in the rear—no doubt chunks of mud or gravel, maybe a rock that had gotten attached somehow. Even so, something was still, most definitely, not "okay." The car no longer purred; it coughed and sputtered—it sounded like somebody puking up his guts. I kept driving for another thirty miles or so, but I was no longer lulled or lost in dream-like reveries. Instead I was talking to the car, begging, pleading with it to stop puking and go back to sounding the way it was supposed to. I glanced at Luis. "Eduardo," he had said, "I am entrusting you with my car." Reluctantly, knowing I had no other choice, I woke him up.

He told me to stop, and we got out and walked around to the rear of the car. And I was appalled. When for Christ's sake would I learn? I should never put myself at the mercy of machines—anything with a motor in it. Under no circumstances! All the hundreds of potholes that Luis had slammed through at eighty miles an hour, but let me go half that fast, and immediately the car plunges into a pit the size of a Bengal tiger trap and the exhaust pipe snaps in two. And Luis—what would he do now? He didn't have any more bullets in his rifle, but he had his .357 Magnum, and of course there was his machete.

"Eduardo, my friend," he said. "Cheer up! Even to the greatest of drivers, even to myself, such things will happen." Incredibly, Luis had recovered his good spirits; in fact, I wondered if he wasn't delirious. After lurching around the car as though drunk, he then drove us the few miles farther to an all-night truck stop outside the settlement of Watson Lake. We'd go back for the broken-off exhaust pipe, but first we needed gas.

~

I ran ahead in the glare of the headlights, Luis's car coughing and chugging behind me. Finally, at last, I'd been given the opportunity to do something I did well. ("Of course I remember you," my old high school track coach had said a few years before when I ran into him in the hometown post office. "You were my sprint man.") If I didn't have any business driving a car through the Yukon night, well, at least I could be out there like I was, running through it.

Or so I might have felt but for why I was out there in the first place. Trying to find that goddamned broken-off exhaust pipe. And chagrined and mortified as I still was, I was determined to keep running up and down that raggedy dark road until I did find it.

Afterward, and after assuring me that the piece of pipe could be welded back on, Luis drove us back to Watson Lake, where we stopped at a roadside inn for breakfast. The inn had all the trappings: log walls, a stuffed, snarling lynx next to the cash register, moose head above a burning fireplace, bear rug in front of it. A motherly waitress bustled about, and a palsied, toothless old man who looked like he might have trekked over the Chilkoot Pass to the Klondike in 1898 sat in his chair by the fire. Blanket on his lap, he listened as Luis described the ordeals of our journey. Lying on the bear rug, I nodded off. Suddenly I heard Luis exclaim, "Oh no, I am serious! You must never pees into the Amazon!"

"Why the hell not?" the old man cried. "Cause I might pollute it? Jesus Christ, you don't mean you've got those goddamned Sierra Clubbers down there, too, telling a man what he can't do."

"No, no," Luis said. "It is because of thees tiny little fish. It is like a toothpick, and it has these sharp fins, like needles, and it will swim up the stream of your pees and into your pee-nis. Then it will plant its fins and you cannot get the fish out."

"Aw, now, I don't know as I believe that or not," the old man grinned.

"Oh yes, it is true," Luis said. "And when this happens, it causes great pain, and you will never make love again."

"Well, hell," the old man said, looking down and giving me a wink, "I don't know as I gotta worry too much about that, anyway."

"You do not believe me," Luis said, "but what I tell you—it is true."

"Maybe so," the old man said, giving me another wink, "but you wanna know something? We've got something up here every bit as bad. Ever hear of the ice snake?"

"Ice snake?"

"Yep, that's what I said. And just let me tell you, it gets to be winter up here and you gotta use the outhouse, you wanta take a flashlight and look real good to make sure there ain't any goddamned ice snake in it before you squat down."

"Why? Because it will bite you?"

"No, worse'n that. It'll crawl up your asshole and freeze you to death," the old man said, sputtering with laughter.

White Horse, capitol of the Yukon Territory. A town of some 5,000 people, 917 miles up the Alaska Highway and only a half-day's drive to the border with Alaska. We roared into White Horse, the Yukon River on our right, at ninety miles an hour. But that was strictly for show. The car was sick, and at the local Volkswagen garage we were told it would take at least two days to repair it. No way, said Luis. That was out of the question. While he was telling people why the repairs had to be done sooner, I left and found us a room at a nearby motel. When I returned, mechanics were already working on the car, with Luis scurrying about like a frantic mother hen, barking orders, giving instructions. I tried to catch his attention, but he was too busy. One of the mechanics told me they hoped to have the car ready by noon the next day.

"That soon," I said.

"Hey, for what it's going to cost your buddy, we'll work all night. Only thing, it'd sure help if he'd stop being such a pain in the ass and let us do our job."

I went back to the motel, eagerly anticipating what was to come: a bath—a steaming, piping-hot bath. Then I crawled into bed—this time a bed of my own. Stretching out my legs, the sheets so clean and cool and white, I thought about the night ahead, Luis with credit cards to burn, and the girls and bars of White Horse. I wished I had something to drink, like a 7-Up and some bourbon. And I wished there were a phone in the room. I wanted so badly to call Louise, hear the sound of her voice. I thought about getting up and going out and finding a bar somewhere and having a couple of drinks. And then calling her. First, though, I needed to get some rest. But no sooner had I drifted off than the bed started moving—and then I was back in the car and we were hurtling down a dark road with potholes the size of manholes. I pulled the sheets up, buried my face in a pillow—finally, the bed stopped moving.

~

Luis stood in front of the mirror, clad in a pair of purple bikini shorts. Already bathed and shaved, he splashed his face and chest with lotions, spurted his armpits and crotch with deodorants, doused himself with talcum.

"Eduardo, get up! The club next door has a group. The piano player, he is terrible, but they have a good drummer, and he says in another hour, perhaps two—that is when the poosee comes. So I will see you there. And us this," he urged waving his bottle of deodorant in front of me as though it were ammonia to revive me. "I tell you, they smell that and they go wild. Believe me."

Garbed in a red bandana, white silk shirt, and black slacks with a tooled, silver-buckled belt, Luis donned his cowboy hat and checked himself out one last time in the mirror. Then, slapping his hand to his hip and executing a fast draw, he was out the door. I thought about getting up to join him, and that was the last I remember.

Late the next morning, after Luis had gotten his car we had breakfast at a downtown café. He told me that the group had let him sit in and play the piano, and that he had danced with many girls. "Ah, Eduardo, had we but one more night—*uno mas noche.*"

He went ahead while I got a cup of coffee for the road. Back on the street I found kids, businessmen, and a cluster of attractive young women—doubtless secretaries on lunch breaks, miniskirted, hair in bouffants—gathered around Luis and his car, the car washed, waxed, and polished, resplendent in the day's bright sun. And Luis, dressed in his black Stetson cowboy hat, shades, black parka with the Laguna Seca patch on the shoulder and the American flag on the breast, Levi's and shiny black boots—he, too, was resplendent.

"Hey, piano player," some fellow who must have seen him perform at the club the night before cried out, "can you sing, too?"

Spreading his legs and snapping his fingers, Luis obliged. "When I was a baby ... Mama told me son ... Always be a good boy ... Don't ever play with guns ... but I shot a man in Reno ... just to watch him ... die." People clapped and cheered, and Luis doffed his Stetson and took a bow. This was his moment. He was the Man in Black, Gaucho from the Pampas, Cisco Kid—the Cowboy of the Western World.

Not far out of town we came to a sign saying ROAD CREW AT WORK. We bashed through piles of gravel and rocks, every jolt and thud seeming more jarring than ever. Which of course only made Luis drive faster, cursing, banging his fists against the steering wheel.

Ahead of us, a grader moved slowly, and a longhaired flag man waved us down. Slamming to a stop, Luis cried to him, "You can see, can't you, what this road is doing to my car!"

"Yeah, yeah, man," the flag man said, nodding agreeably. "I hear what you're saying. Hey, you dudes wouldn't have any dope on you, would you? Yeah, man, I just ran out, thought you might have some . . . Well, hey, man, that's cool, maybe the next dude who comes along. Take it slow," he said, flagging us on.

Luis, of course, didn't "take it slow," at least not for the next fifty miles or so. When we heard a new scraping. Only this time it wasn't from the rear. This time it was the front fenders that had been shaken loose and were cutting into his tires. Furiously, Luis took off his racing tires and put on his standards. But the fenders still looked like they were about to fall off, and loose as they were, it wouldn't take too many more bumps before they'd be cutting into the smaller tires.

We got back in the car. Luis sat shaking his head and biting his lips. "This son-of-a-bitching road! I tell you, you can believe me—this is a goddamned motherfucking son-of-a-bitching road!" He sighed, fingers drumming against the steering wheel. He lit a cigarette, took a puff, again sighed and shook his head, fingers still drumming. Then he started the car.

"Well, my friend," he said, turning to me with a grin, "now, perhaps we will enjoy the scenic vistas, okay?"

He drove on at a sane, measured, leisurely pace, and for the first time since we had left Dawson Creek I was actually seeing the country. Albeit under a clouded sky and through intermittent showers of rain. We passed vast areas of burned-out timber, of charred stumps and blackened trees with shriveled spidery limbs sticking up like unholy scarecrows, the roadside aflame with beds of fireweed. Then Kluane Lake, the biggest lake in the Yukon Territory, its surface a translucent turquoise green, its 600-foot depths reputedly inhabited by giant land-locked sea serpents—and, if not, well, *Ursus horribilis* haunted its rugged shorelines, and that would more than do.

More rain. The road became a network of small streams glittering in the afternoon's surreal light. With a great brooding, cloud-shrouded mountain wall rearing up before us, tentacles of mist curling down its slopes. We crossed a bridge over the White River, only the water wasn't white but coffee-brown from glacial silt. Two moose appeared on a sandbar, browsing on willow. Luis stopped the car and got out to stalk them with his camera, the moose browsing on, unconcerned, contented as cows.

Only once did Luis revert to old form, and that was when a car tried to pass. Fenders might fall and tires be reduced to rubbery confetti, but nobody was going to make him eat dust.

"My friend, you must believe me, I promise you—no way."

Then—at last, Alaska, and right on cue, the rain stopped falling, and we were once more on pavement. Then we went through customs and after that came to Tok Junction, where one road went to Anchorage, the other to Fairbanks. Luis pulled his car over, and I got out. We shook hands, and said whatever it was we said. Then, peeling tires, dust, and gravel flying in his wake, Luis drove off.

And abruptly as he had come into my life, he was gone. Luis Garcia Mendoza. Often, when I've tried to describe him to people over the years, I've either made him out to be a colorful character or a dreadful, awful person. Or sometimes both. When of course, actually, he was really neither. Like myself, he simply ran his heedless ways.

Meanwhile, there "on the pavements gray," some part of me still stands. Back in a time when so much of the road still lie ahead rather than behind.

Not Telling Anything New
CHARLOTTE MATTHEWS

You probably know
this is a box of gold,
woman throwing ashes
on the turned garden,
the snow that comes down,
wind soughing the meadow

I am trying to see things as they are
but the moon might disappear
while you are looking, the ocean
cease to dwell in the sea
glass you hold.

I was afraid of losing him
and it happened.

Leaves decompose
in water the rain left,
tiny punched holes
elaborate as lace.

The only way I know
how to say this
is still not right.

I saw a bird carry her daughter
over the Great Strand River.

It gets cold. It gets dark.

There are bright specks on the snow.
Come, quick, before they fly away.

Famine Roads
GRETCHEN STEELE

Galway, Ireland: September 2001

Across Galway Bay,
crumbling limestone roads
still cling halfway up the steep Burren,
Irish for 'a stony place.'
Relief work for Famine victims—
building roads to nowhere.
From sea level in Kinvarna,
hauling slabs of karstic limestone
from the shattered acres
of Rockforest,
a few yards every day for years
up the side of Mullaghmore Mountain
toward Black Head.

They clambered in the sludge,
clutching each stone into place,
cheeks laid on wet limestone,
hugging the hillside
like the low tufts of purple heather.
Below, the Atlantic meets the cliffs
with no room for beach. Canyons
of dark water.
Across Galway Bay, I take pictures
of the place they dropped
their picks and shovels, unfolded
cramped hands, let go.

How does sadness become holy ground?
I found myself on the steps
of an overflowing cathedral there

one Sunday in September,
all the shops closed.
Outside, none of us looked away
when our eyes met. Outside,
it was a day on the edge
of not being a day. The damp smell
of hymnals and incense sifting down
through the open doors was enough
to remind us of something
we hadn't done in a long time,
enough to keep us there as the rain
came in at us sideways.

The Pattern of Life Indelible
ROBERT ROOT

A lake is the landscape's most beautiful and expressive feature. It is earth's eye; looking into which the beholder measures the depth of his own nature.

—Henry David Thoreau, *Walden*

I. GREAT POND 2002

I am surprised when I reach the end of the road. Strolling casually through Bear Springs Camp, gazing at the backs of cabins and glimpsing Great Pond beyond them, I expected to find a footpath through the woods, some way to keep following the shoreline. But I see only thick woods and dense undergrowth straight ahead. Knowing I have to retrace my steps, I glance longingly towards the shoreline, but the cabins are close together and I'm reluctant to walk between them to reach it, timid about blundering into someone's privacy. Two cars with New Jersey plates are parked under the trees behind the last cabin. Where I find cars I will likely find people in the cabin or on the porch or at the water's edge. Boats tied up to the docks in front of each cabin also suggest that people are still around and even earlier, when I passed a cabin without cars, I heard a baby fussing inside. Finding no trail into the woods and no unobtrusive path to the shoreline, I turn back the way I came.

A dozen yards ahead a woman is standing in the middle of the dirt road, looking at me. We passed each other only a moment or two earlier, her brief "Guh mawning" linking her to the Jersey plates and the last cabin. She waits as I amble toward her and before I am very near asks if I'm looking for someone. I say no, just wandering. She asks if I'm staying here, at Bear Springs Camp. This is inland Maine, where folks are relaxed and friendly, but she's from New Jersey and prudently curious about strangers in the neighborhood with no apparent reason for being there. I say, "No, I'm not, but I'm trying to decide if I'd like to stay here next year." This is true but not the whole truth—I don't want to explain that I want to write about the place and that I'm here now because sixty years earlier E. B. White wrote about his own sum-mers on this lake—and I hope my genuine desire to one day be a renter reassures her.

During this exchange, I come almost even with her. She turns and we start walking slowly together, back toward the center of camp. She is a soft, auburn-haired, pale-skinned woman in a striped short-sleeve pullover and dark blue shorts and sandals; I guess that she is some-where in her late forties, maybe early fifties. She encourages me to rent a cabin—"This is a great place and you would love it." I ask if she's stayed at the camp before.

It turns out that she has been coming every year for two decades. Her daughter is twenty-five and "we've been coming since she's five." Many of the other families here this week are people she has known for years, including friends of her children whom they see only at the camp when these far-flung families turn up once a year to stay for the same week in the same cabins. She tells me it's nice to go up to meals (they're on the "American Plan" here, three communal meals a day) and sit at a big table with other campers—"It's like a big family gathering. You get to know people." She says, "At the end of the week, when we leave, we book the cabin for the next year." I wonder aloud if that's why it's so hard to reserve a cabin.

She explains that some people she's met here have been coming for thirty or forty years. The kids keep coming even after they grow up, and when one generation stops coming the family still reserves a cabin and the next generation shows up with children of their own. "There's death, you know, and people divorce, and they get too old, but that's the only thing that opens up spots," she says. "The turnover is small. If you really want to come, put your name on Peg's list and when some-one cancels, then you can get in."

She points me toward the main beach, which I claim to be looking for, and indicates Peg's office in the other direction. Then she smiles and waves and ambles off to meet a friend from another cabin. I look up the dirt road and see my car parked on the side of the blacktop road, opposite the large white building housing the office and the dining hall and the separate little building with the guest laundry. Earlier, to get to the cabins, I followed the dirt road down the slope, gradual, grassy, open, and took the right fork when the road neared the shoreline. I strolled behind the cabins, under hemlocks, spruces, birches, aspen, the woods close and overgrown and the underbrush too dense to tramp through. On the shaded dirt road campers from the cabins scuffing out in the opposite direction occasionally greeted me, and I tried to make my ambling match the easy, unhurried pace of the people I passed, the pace of the life in the camp.

The cabins varied little, from duplexes to single units, some exteriors sided with logs and others with planks, but the roofs always sheet metal and the color of the cabin walls always a dark woodsy brown, freshly repainted. All the cabins had roofed porches and docks and a little bit of green space between the cabin and the lake. Trees that mostly shaded them from the sun on the lakeside were tall and close by the cabins. On the western, landward side of the peninsula, where the woods were thick and usually dark, the cabins were invisible from the blacktop road and blocked from the sun in the afternoon. I thought that darkness must come early here, the sun disappearing behind the trees and the distant western hills long before it disappears from the sky.

I follow the road down to the beach, settle onto a clump of sandy grass under a tree, very near the water, and take my daybook and pen out of my fanny pack. A rivulet running through the camp, shaded near the shoreline and crossed by a little bridge, curves around in front of me and disappears under the plywood dock a few feet away. I've located myself out of the way of the swimming area, near a red plastic paddle boat. Beached sailboats, inflatable dinghies, and kayaks line the shore in one direction and in the other direction I can see a yellow version of the paddleboat and beyond it a large yellow inner tube. Three aluminum rowboats with outboard motors, all bearing the Bears Springs Camp insignia, are tied up to the dock in front of me and a low runabout with a huge Yamaha outboard is moored at the end. I try to blend in with the setting, appear to be an idler from one of the cabins rather than an intruder who hasn't paid for this view. Soon I disappear into the landscape and the pattern of life in the center of the camp reveals itself all around me.

Three young girls stroll along the beach in front of me, pausing to try to break open a mussel with a stone. No luck. After the girls move on three young black ducks pass me, two floating down the rivulet, one waddling on the sand near the lake. Neither preoccupied trio shows any interest in my presence.

In the swimming area two children play with scuba masks while a man videotapes them. Beyond him an older couple, both thick and white-haired, pull a blue cover over the hatch of their white speed boat. Out beyond the swimming area, on an anchored raft almost directly ahead of me, a slim, dark-haired, teenaged girl in a blue one-piece swimsuit shifts from sitting up and leaning back on her hands to lying down and bracing herself on her elbows. Two younger girls skim down the coast in a two-person kayak, working vigorously. A mother and her very young daughter enter the water, the woman dragging an inflated plastic lounge chair, the girl dragging a large yellow inflated octopus with a fixed smile. Two middle aged men, gray and soft, and two younger men, tanned and lean, wade out from the beach and begin playing catch with a large floating dart, which, when they throw it just the right way, makes a ringing noise like a cell phone; perhaps it is a comforting, reassuring sound to some of the people playing. The mother and daughter return to the shore, both smiling, the octopus still wearing its goofy grin. Another black duck wanders toward me, honking all the way, gets within a foot and a half before turning back. Three docks away two people board a blocky pontoon boat, with an awning covering the rear half.

The sky is hazy, the air humid, but the wind is brisk and cooling despite its warmth. The camp curves around the shoreline, facing mostly east and southeast, near the base of the peninsula stretching south into Great Pond toward Jamaica Point. The haze obscures the distant shores of Great Pond—only the near shoreline appears as a vivid green. The islands in the lake, the eastern shore, the hills beyond are lighter and lighter shades of blue. Pale blue sky breaks through the haze sometimes but though the sun is high now, as it nears midday, the shadows are seldom sharp or well-defined. It is supposed to rain today but I see nothing moving in yet.

On most of the cabin porches beach towels, swimsuits, T-shirts and similar colorful summerwear hang drying in the breeze (though not often in the sun). I can see a porch across the clearing where red, white, yellow, blue, green strips of cloth are draped on the railing, pennants signalling family presence to those offshore. In the other direction the cabin three docks over has a clothesline on the far end of the porch, white plastic chairs and table taking up most of the floor space, and a pile of bright plastic inflatable water toys—rafts, dinghies, octopus, floating loungechair—piled against the wall.

The men in the swimming area pursue their dart-catching game as far out as the raft and then end it to paddle around some and chat as they drift toward shore. In the distance I can hear the sound of jet skis—one is hurtling through the water towing a raft with someone lying prone hanging on to it. The runabout at the end of the near dock has gone out near a double kayak and someone leaps from the boat and joins another young man in the kayak. On shore some people sit in a circle, slumped in white plastic chairs, conversing. In the distance I see a group of laughing women in lounge chairs and another group chatting on the cabin steps.

Peace and goodness and jollity, White called it, summertime, oh, summertime, pattern of life indelible. The only urgency is in the jet skis, and urgency is their nature, their reason for being—who rides a jet ski to be leisurely with their leisure time? Even the two men in the double kayak are being towed by the runabout, defeating the point of kayaking, I would guess. And yet it's all to pass the time, to do little that requires doing, to rest in between bouts of playing and relaxing and socializing, to feel that even urgency here is a form of play when it shows up.

As noon approaches and the sky hazes over more the beach empties. I notice an osprey hovering above the lake and follow him with field glasses as he glides toward the peninsula, coming to rest on a high branch of a tree along the shore. From time to time I check to see if he, too, will join the activity on the lake. Except for the black ducks and chickadees calling in the distance and an occasional swallow darting out over the water I haven't seen any other bird activity. Surely there are more birds in all this bug-filled forest. Then the osprey is gone and takes with him my sudden interest in birdwatching. I rise creakily after two hours in one cross-legged position and limber up slowly. As I follow the dirt road up the slope I notice that the building where the campers gather for the midday meal is busy and the cabins behind me are quiet. Knowing that I'm going to my car instead of a communal meal makes me again aware that I am an outsider at Bear Springs Camp. But then why, I wonder, do I feel so comfortable here?

II. ONCE MORE TO THE LAKE 1941

E. B. White was someone who came often to Great Pond. As he says in the opening of his essay, "Once More to the Lake": "One summer, along about 1904, my father rented a camp on a lake in Maine and took us all there for the month of August. We all got ringworm from some kittens and had to rub Pond's Extract on our arms and legs night and morning, and my father rolled over in a canoe with all his clothes on; but outside of that the vacation was a success, and from then on none of us ever thought there was a place in the world like that lake in Maine." His account of his first visit reads with the breathlessness of a child eager to get in everything in one telling, but as the essay progresses he reveals that he is writing now about a visit to the pond he made with his own son and how finding himself in the role of father in a place where he was accustomed to the role of son confused him about the immediacy of the past and the present. It seems to him that he is reliving his own childhood rather than simply witnessing his son's experience of the camp—"I seemed to be living a dual existence. I would be in the middle of some simple act, I would be picking up a bait box or laying down a table fork, or I would be saying something, and suddenly it would be not I but my father who was saying the words or making the gesture. It gave me a creepy sensation." He sees a dragonfly alight on the tip of his fishing rod. "It was the arrival of this fly that convinced me beyond any doubt that everything was as it had always been, that the years were a mirage and there had been no years." Everything he sees around him he feels he has seen before and when he dislodges the dragonfly as he had in childhood, he repeats himself: "There had been no years between the ducking of this dragonfly and the other one—the one that was part of memory." He sees one of the campers in the water with a cake of soap, "and the water felt thin and clear and unsubstantial. Over the years there had been this person with the cake of soap, this cultist, and here he was. There had been no years."

The changes White does observe and record are seemingly slight—the old three-track dirt road of the horse-drawn wagons is now a two-track of automobiles; the waitresses in the farmhouse dining room have cleaner hair, like girls in movies; there are louder, larger motors on the boats and more Coca Cola, less sarsparilla, birch beer, and Moxie in the little general store—but nonetheless they indicate a passage of time that so much of the experience of the place seems to deny. "There had been no years," he says, and "it was all the same." He virtually chants: "Summertime, oh, summertime, pattern of life indelible, the fadeproof lake, the woods unshatterable, the pasture with the sweetfern and the juniper forever and ever, summer without end; this was the background, and the life along the shore was the design, the cottages with their innocent and tranquil design, their tiny docks with the flagpole and the American flag floating against the white clouds in the blue sky, the little paths over the roots of the trees leading from camp to camp and the path leading back to the outhouses and the can of lime for sprinkling, and at the souvenir counters at the store the miniature birch-bark canoes and the post cards that showed things looking a little better than they looked."

Toward the end of the essay White gives an overview of what their week was like: "The bass were biting well and the sun shone endlessly, day after day. We would be tired at night and lie down in the accumulated heat of the little bedrooms after the long hot day and the breeze would stir almost imperceptibly outside and the smell of the swamp drift in through the rusty screens." All of this stirs his memory with Proustian clarity and detail—"I kept remembering everything, lying in bed in the morning"—and as they continue doing things together and this long paragraph is filled with the first-person plural ("We would go up to the store. . . . We would walk out. . . . We explored the streams . . . we lay on the town wharf . . .") he declares: "Everywhere we went I had trouble making out which was I, the one walking at my side, the one walking in my pants."

Then there is a long paragraph with a single "I" in it ("like the revival of an old melodrama that I had seen long ago") describing a kind of universal summer thunderstorm. "The second-act climax of the drama of the electrical disturbance over a lake in America had not changed in any important respect. This was the big scene, still the big scene." He describes the storm: "The whole thing was so familiar, the first feeling of oppression and heat and a general air around camp of not wanting to go very far away. In midafternoon (it was all the same) a curious darkening of the sky, and a lull in everything that had made life tick." It's as if the narrator draws back from his own experience by leaving out verbs and actors until the storm begins to abate, and even then he refers to the campers generally, "running out in joy and relief to go swimming in the rain, their bright cries perpetuating the deathless joke about how they were getting simply drenched, and the children screaming with delight at the new sensation of bathing in the rain, and the joke about getting drenched linking the generations in a strong indestructible chain. And the comedian who waded in carrying an umbrella."

But then he tells us that his son decides to join the swimmers and takes down his rain-soaked trunks from the clothesline. "Languidly, and with no thought of going in, I watched him, his hard little body, skinny and bare, saw him wince slightly as he pulled up around his vitals the small, soggy, icy garment. As he buckled the swollen belt, suddenly my groin felt the chill of death."

I don't know how many times now I have read and reread the essay, but the way it leads us gullibly, serenely toward the conclusion always affects me, always makes me feel a jolt at the concluding paragraph, always make me look back at all those instances where there was foreshadowing or foreboding—"perpetuating the deathless joke," for instance, or the generations linked "in a strong, indestructible chain." This is essay as lyric, as elegy on a theme of mutability, both as plainspoken and as poetic as the "language men do use" in a Wordsworthian ode. When we consider the music of its language, its rhythms and repetitions, and the way it is as cunningly crafted as a Hemingway short story, both in language and in emotion, it's easy to agree with the essayist Joseph Epstein that "Once More to the Lake" is "dazzling and devastating, art of a heightened kind that an essayist is rarely privileged to achieve."

iii. The Rain in Maine 2002

Because Bear Springs Camp had been booked all month, we were staying in a bed-and-breakfast in the village of Belgrade Lakes, located on a narrow strip of land between Great Pond to the east and Long Pond to the west. When I drove back from the camp on the North Bay of Great Pond, I found my wife working on research on the screened-in, backward-L-shaped porch on the western front on the inn. We put our notebooks away and changed our clothes to go canoeing and as we stepped outside the thunder that had been booming faintly in the east grew louder and the sky darkened. On the front doorstep of the inn, just as we changed the plan to a walk down to a tavern, the wind picked up and the innkeeper, who had just begun to mow the lawn, wheeled the riding mower around and headed back to the barn and the wind gusted strongly and we went back inside and settled back on the porch. Within minutes the storm was upon us, the peals of thunder regular and almost deafening, the lightning less noticeable through all the trees except when it flashed close enough, the boom following immediately, that we were sure it had struck down by the water.

The wind grew less persistent and gusty but the rain came thick and hard. We sat on the screened-in porch and listened to it churn and hiss and splatter, watched it drop on two sides of us as if we were sitting behind an L-shaped waterfall. The thunder rumbled deep after every boom, rolled off into the distance. The south side of the house had a narrow strip of garden and a little way beyond it a wall of tall thick maples shielding the house from the town, so we couldn't see very deeply into the storm. On the west side, the usual view of an open lawn and a scattering of older, larger trees, lawn furniture, a wishing well, a stand of wood lilies, was nearly invisible behind the translucent rain-beaded screen.

As White had written, "This was the big scene, still the big scene," and the thunder seemed to be playing the score for percussion as he had described it: " . . . the premonitory rumble. Then the kettle drum, then the snare, then the bass drum and cymbals . . . " Listening to the whole orchestration of storm, I wondered about the people at Bear Springs Camp, imagined them huddled in their cabins, the rain heavier and closer on their metal roofs, lake and sky merging in one liquid flow, the air thick with the windows closed but cooling where the screen door protected by the porch roof would be open.

The storm rumbled persistently as it passed, and then the rain lessened and the sky to the west brightened and the beads in the front screen began to disintegrate of their own weight so that the view cleared somewhat. Unseen traffic on the road in front of the yard now sometimes drowned out the sounds of the storm. Bird calls came again and with the brightening sky the return of shadows. And then, while the trees and the roofs continued to drip, the storm was over.

Later, after dinner, sitting out on the porch, we noticed the gleaming sky. It was sunset but the glow was so bright that we strolled down to Peninsula Park across the street for a clear, unobstructed view across Long Pond of the spectacular sky. The pond was a deep blue tending toward black, the hills along the distant shore were black, but behind the hills the sky was on fire, dazzlingly golden, gleaming yellow-orange and tinting the clouds pink and red. To the north some clouds shaped like mountain ranges hung in dark blue against the blue-gray of the night sky and between them and us lower translucent clouds hung like ponds at the base of hills. We could see the dark clouds through the transparent clouds and they seemed to be casting their shadows on water, like the real hills and real shadows and real water below. At times the mountain range clouds would rise enough so that they seemed a distant range with a bank of fog filling the intervening valley. Then a cool breeze picked up, and as the sun, invisible in the west, sank lower, it pulled the golden sky after it like a curtain.

IV. ONCE MORE TO THE LAKE 1941

When I look at "Once More to the Lake" as an essay of place,—as, that is, an essay in which the evocation of setting is central to the development of theme or character or action—I am aware of how much it is suffused by the author's familiarity with the landscape and the routine behaviors of the people who have populated it over time. White is a significantly elegaic essayist, the darkness or brooding undercurrent that many of his critics have noted in his amiable pose as an temperate observer of the everyday often growing out of his awareness of time passing and his distrust of headlong, intemperate change. Not only his frequent returns to Great Pond but also his long residency near a small, out-of-the-way Maine village attest to his preference for a relatively simple, relatively repetitive lifestyle (a word I'm sure he would never willingly use). One of the hallmarks of the nonfiction of place is its success in evoking in the reader familiar with the setting a recognition, sometimes uncomfortable, of the accuracy and insight of the recreation—it may be inevitable that some readers will disagree with the essayist's interpretation of life in that setting, but they will still be able to say, "Yes, I know this place; this account is true to the place where I live." A second, connected hallmark of the nonfiction of place is its ability to trigger in the reader *unfamiliar* with the setting a similar sense of having been there, to provoke the ability to dwell within the textual place. This is, after all, what armchair travelers are seeking to achieve, a sense of having lived in a space they have never inhabited except vicariously. I would argue that, in the most successful nonfiction of place, both kinds of readers, insiders and outsiders, feel they are in the same space, feel they would know the space again if they visited it.

The intimacy that the writer evidences with the place in the essay arises from long familiarity with it. According to his biographer, White came with his family to Belgrade Lakes for the first time in August 1905 (not 1904), and the annual monthly stay at a camp on Great Pond continued for several years. In 1914 White took a friend, Frederick Schuler, to Snug Harbor Camps and wrote and illustrated a pamphlet for Freddie describing the place. As an adult he returned to Great Pond and stayed at Bert Mosher's Bear Springs Camp on his own—for example, he abruptly disappeared from his job at the *New Yorker* in September of 1927 and wrote his editor from Belgrade, and in January 1929 he stayed with Bert Mosher and iceskated on Great Pond. In 1936, shortly after his mother died in May and nearly a year after his father's death in August 1935, he wrote to his brother Stanley from Bert Mosher's camp. Stanley was eight years older and had been White's most important playmate during the early days in Maine. The letter to Stanley suggests that White's association of Belgrade Lakes with changelessness was connected with intimate and inevitable issues of mortality raised by the loss of their parents, but that White, who to that point had never written essays expressly about his personal life, wasn't ready to deal with these issues in a public piece of writing. Yet the letter to Stanley establishes a pattern of thematic repetition that would surface later in "Once More to the Lake."

He started the letter: "I returned to Belgrade. Things haven't changed much." On the Bar Harbor Express, "when you look out of the window in the diner, steam is rising from the pastures and the sun is out, and pretty soon the train is skirting a blue lake called Messalonski. Things don't change much." The letter continues a litany of description in present tense: "The lake hangs clear and still at dawn . . . In the shallows along shore the pebbles and driftwood show clear and smooth on bottom, and black water bugs dart, spreading a wake and a shadow . . . The water in the basin is icy before breakfast, and cuts sharply into your nose and ears and makes your face blue as you wash. . . . The insides of your camp are hung with pictures cut from magazines, and the camp smells of lumber and damp. Things don't change much." The letter is one long paragraph of description, recounting in detail the continuous present. "You buy a drink of Birch Beer at Bean's tackle store. Big bass swim lazily in the deep water at the end of the wharf, well fed. Long lean guide boats kick white water in the stern until they suck under. There are still one cylinder engines that don't go. Maybe it's the needle valve." He concludes: "Yes, sir, I returned to Belgrade, and things don't change much. I thought somebody ought to know."

By the time White went once more to the lake with his son, Joel, in July 1941, he was writing a monthly column for *Harper's Magazine* called "One Man's Meat" that required him to regularly fill a designated space in the magazine. On July 24 he wrote his wife, Katharine, that "Joe has been in [the lake] for more than an hour without showing the slightest tendency to come out. He is a devotee of fresh water swimming at the moment, and it really does seem good to have warm bathing for a change." He explained what they had been doing and how they had "a perfectly enormous outboard motor on our rowboat" which he had difficulty starting and which lurched up to speed with jarring power. "I miss the old one-cylinder gas engine of yesteryear which made a fine peaceful sound across the water. This is too much like living on the edge of an airfield." But nonetheless he was enthusiastic about being there. "This place is as American as a drink of Coca-Cola. The white collar family having its annual liberty. I must say it seems sort of good. . . . Everybody you've ever seen on Main Street or on Elm Avenue is here."

These two letters foreshadow much of the language and many of the subthemes of "Once More to the Lake." For example, in the opening paragraphs he mentions the "fearful cold of the sea-water" making him long for "the placidity of a lake in the woods" and how his son "had never had any fresh water up his nose." His mantra from the letter to Stanley changes only slightly ("there had been no years"; "it was all the same."), and his descriptions echo earlier ones: "In the shallows, the dark, watersoaked sticks and twigs, smooth and old, were undulating in clusters on the bottom against the clean ribbed sand, and the track of the mussel was plain." Or: "My boy loved our rented outboard, and his great desire was to achieve singlehanded mastery over it, and authority, and he soon learned the trick of choking it a little (but not too much), and the adjustment of the needle valve." The language is more deliberately chosen and its rhythms more carefully modulated—White claimed to write by ear and his manuscripts show the effort to revise for sound and pace—but again and again the earlier letters echo in the essay.

Whether White consulted the letters again before writing the essay or not—as any journalkeeper knows, transcribing your thoughts often

L1C0

locks them in your memory in retrievable form—one of the distinguishing qualities of this essay is its long gestation period. White was forty-two when he wrote it (it was submitted to the magazine for its August 1941 deadline and published untitled in the "One Man's Meat" department in October 1941), and he had been observing Great Pond and rehearsing his reflections upon it for at least thirty-six years. Perhaps, in addition to its affecting power, what contributes greatly to the sense of place which underlies the essay is its aura of lived experience, its simultaneous superimposition of place and persona on the page. In the nonfiction of place the author's persona is not simply situated in place; more compellingly, place is situated within—and emerges from—the author.

v. GREAT POND 2002

On our final morning at Belgrade Lakes, I went out to visit the camp one last time. In the interval between my first visit and my last I had taken in the terrain from a couple of different levels. I had climbed a few local mountains in search of an overview of the landscape and seen northwoods forest sweeping away in every direction, open to the sky only where the ponds were. I knew this impression of vast wilderness was illusory; White himself says of Great Pond, "The lake had not been what you would call a wild lake. There were cottages sprinkled around the shores, and it was in farming country, although the shores of the lake were heavily wooded." I knew that the camp itself had been constructed on a farm and, as with so many camps of this kind, the farmhouse served as the office and communal dining hall and operations center. For much of the early part of the twentieth century, when there were many camps on the Maine lakes, the camps were a way for the farmers to diversify and subsidize their farming. Now most of the camps were gone and Bear Springs Camp was one of the few still operating pretty much as it had operated, improvements in plumbing and accessibility and leisure toy construction being the principle variables. Across Maine, across New England, in the decline of farming, in the wake of emigration westward, the forests had returned and now feigned permanence, immutability. When we left Belgrade Lakes we would drive only twenty miles or so, to Vienna (pronounced "VYE-enna"), to watch friends celebrate the village's bicentennial and to walk the woods of their lot, much of which had been field, pasture, and woodlot two hundred years ago.

We had also seen Great Pond from lake level. We rented a canoe from an outfitter on the quiet waterway that cuts through the village of Belgrade Lakes and connects Long Pond to Great Pond and paddled out onto Great Pond. The lake itself was moderately choppy and wind-swept, and we had to paddle continuously to gain ground, staying near the shore, running out into the lake only to avoid docks and rafts and anchored boats and empty anchors and, occasionally, shoals. It was surprisingly quiet much of the time—occasionally someone would speed through the center of the lake and we would contend with mild wakes or a pontoon boat would charge away from the dock in front of someone's house, but most of the time we saw nobody but an older woman reading a novel on her dock and a few elderly people sitting on lounge chairs under an umbrella or, toward the end of our outing, four youngsters in kayaks venturing out from their cottage while someone's father stopped reading on the dock long enough to tie up the dogs that kept jumping in the water trying to follow the kids.

It had been good to see the shoreline from the lake, though we didn't go around to Bear Springs Camp but only tested the waters. These were mostly private homes, perhaps a few inns or B&Bs or rent-als, no camps, but the well-to-do who could afford these places seemed to me to not be moved by much different desires than the people at Bear Springs Camp—the desire to relax, to get away, to luxuriate in down-time. The upscale private cottages were no doubt further upscale than they had been sixty years earlier, but the "American family taking its annual liberty" on Great Pond seemed to have largely maintained the same demographics as in White's experience.

To wind things up, I felt I needed to circumnavigate Great Pond by car, so I drove south first, then rounded the southern end and followed the road up the east side in search of Horse Point Road and a view of North Bay. At a Boy Scout camp at the end of the road I gazed through binoculars at Bear Springs Camp across the bay, idling in the sun, the woods rising behind it. It seemed a small narrow strip between the wide strips of blue sky, green forest, blue lake, completely insignificant from the opposite shoreline and probably content to be inconspicuous, unlike some of the private homes further out on Jamaica Point. When I stopped at a higher point along the road, overlooking a busy quarry digging away the side of the hill, I couldn't see the camp at all.

I circled back around to the camp then, parked on the road in the same shady spot I had before, and walked down the dirt road to the central beach. It was a cooler day and the beach was less active than it had been, though I was there around the same time of day. Boys were hitting golf-ball- and softball-sized whiffleballs and a woman in a swimsuit was taking pictures of her family in front of their cabin, but no one was in the water except for a middle-aged man who took out a kayak as I arrived and, in the distance, a single fisherman and one lone jet skier. In front of the beachfront cabins there were a few idlers but not much was going on.

The sky was a perfect blue with perfectly wispy clouds to break up that unblemished blue. The wind was very light and the water the same blue as the sky, the same placid attitude. From the end of the dock I took pictures of North Bay, of the shoreline, of the gigantic spruce that must be the oldest tree on the farm, of the creek winding through the sand to empty on the beach. Then I took my time walking back up the road toward the office-farmhouse-dining hall. Two teenage girls were taking turns with the payphone at the end of the porch, one of them someone I had seen earlier near the cabins, talking on a cellphone. Peg Churchill and her mother and two daughters were in the office, not doing much. Peg was pleasant, polite, but reserved. I told her who I was and why I was there and she seemed content to show no reaction or interest. In order to seem to have more purpose in my presence I asked if I could see a photo of E. B. White that I had read about in an article about the place, and she went in the family room to get it.

The picture is a five-by-seven-inch blowup from a snapshot and shows White, perhaps in his eighties or late seventies at the youngest, pulling away from shore in his canoe. He is thin but barrel-chested, his plaid short-sleeved shirt unbuttoned, exposing his white chest and stomach, his tan or beige shorts almost matching his white legs. He is sockless, wearing sneakers or deck shoes, and he has a billed cap on his head and sunglasses. He seems energetic, if not strong, and concentrates on paddling the canoe. One of the cabins and a dock and a stretch of shoreline make up the background of the picture. He could be any other camper, simply engaged in a commonplace leisure activity.

I thanked her for the look at the picture, tried vainly to lure her into small talk, failed, and departed. Outside I ran into the woman from New Jersey coming from the guest laundry. She asked if I had any luck getting a reservation, then told me as we parted that she and her family would be here another week before they went back. As I walked back to my car, I thought, perhaps zanily, that I at least knew something of what it was to spend time here, connect to people, and depart. In spite of the interval of time and the circumstances of my presence here, I had been to E. B. White's Great Pond. (It was all the same.) Thanks to his essay, and the refusal of the place itself to change very much, I, who had never been here before, had come once more to the lake.

Engine Room
DAVID RIVARD

What if the aging bureaucrat a department-head
in mussy gray tweed sportscoat, with gold napkin
and button-down blue Oxford
his receding afro gray-freaked & tightly clipped
what if he sits alone
on a park bench across the street
tapping the fingers of his left hand
on the so-called bottom-line
the Center for Tobacco Control's 2005 Budget unstable in his lap
while the blood-orange oriole
machine-embroidered onto his baseball cap
watches or appears to watch at any rate
a green fly folding & unfolding its languorously iridescent wings
right there on the brim
that's the way it looks
this close to a man's thoughts
as soon as they have been provided with a nickname
the nickname he'd assumed so eagerly
during those years in the engine room
but to become another person
how could that be possible
while the destroyer sailed in humid coastal waters
he remembers he gave blood once
to save a blond gunner's mate
a Kansan who spoke of daddy's girls
curfewed girls & muddy hymnals
he liked to tell of choirs singing for rain
when the devil's hand mirror appeared in the sky
two hours later he was dead
there on the boat where it mattered most

that you wake up breathing hard & fast
when the order was given
"Come here," says a voice in the distance
a woman in blue culottes & halter top swiveling near a tot lot
"I'm serious," she says to a crying toddler
"Come here now."

Eye of the Sanderling
ALAN POOLE

*The sanderling is the white sandpiper or "peep" of summer beaches,
the tireless toy bird that runs before the surf. Because of the bold role
it plays in its immense surroundings, it is the one sandpiper that
most people have noticed. Yet how few notice it at all, and few of the
fewer still who recognize it will ever ask themselves why it is there
or where it might be going ....*

— Peter Matthiessen, "The Wind Birds"

I see them first as a faint rippling in the sand, the smooth wet sand left
behind as the waves retreat. My beachgoing reverie, nourished in part
by the sheen of sunlight on that ribbon of ocean edge, is shaken ever
so slightly as that sheen wrinkles an instant before the next wave slides
up the beach to erase it. Wading into the water I see a few gray shells
tumbling in the surf; my curiosity aroused, I dig into the soft wet sand
and lift a handful.

Instantly my hand comes alive: no dull, inert sand here, but a
hundred kicking legs, digging into my fingers, tunneling, scratching,
desperate to escape. Mole crabs! *Emerita talpoida*—egg-shaped, sand-
colored creatures, not crab-like at all but domed and rounded like
miniature VW bugs, perfectly shaped for burrowing in the sand, varying in size from barely visible to almost the size of a quarter, "living in
the turmoil of broken waves on sandy beaches, moving up and down
the beach with the tide, and . . . feeding on organic debris caught by
feathery antenna," as K. L. Gosner so aptly summarizes this odd life
in his *Field Guide to the Atlantic Seashore*. With dozens of mole crabs in
each square foot of sand, filtering each retreating wave with "feathery antenna," no wonder the sand wrinkles and winks in the sun.
It's alive . . .

One of the unbroken rules of nature is that protein in abundance
will be used. I drop my handful of mole crabs, see them disappear in
a flash—scrambling gratefully back into the sand—and look ahead.
A warm August beach stretches into the distance, holding just a few
human swimmers and clusters of small birds, all seemingly chasing

the waves. But the birds look more purposeful, more intent. I lift binoculars and watch. Their legs spinning beneath them, these small white sandpipers work the edge of the surf with urgency and precision, staying just above the breaking waves, darting down as a wave retreats, fast beaks probing the wet sand like sewing machines, zipping back up ahead of foam and water. Not one gets drenched, barely wet even except for feet and legs, and from time to time one emerges with a smooth gray pebble in its beak, or so it seems. But I know better now, especially when I see that pebble worried in the beak, then swallowed fast and furtively before the chase resumes.

Who are they, these diminutive white shorebirds that materialize suddenly each July and August along Atlantic beaches to glut on mole crabs, only to disappear—most of them—with the first cold winds of fall? What is the world their eye takes in? Sanderlings (*Calidris alba*) are among the most widespread of sandpipers, a group noted for spanning the globe in migration. Here in North America, the species breeds on high arctic tundra from the Alaskan coastal plain across an immense sweep of remote northern Canadian islands to Greenland. From there, seeking similar barren tundra, they scatter east, circling back around the northern extremes through Spitsbergen (Norway), Russia (Taymyr Peninsula, Severnaya Zemlya), and the Siberian arctic coast.

Summer is brief at these remote latitudes. By early June, when Sanderlings arrive to court and lay eggs, daylight is constant but snowstorms are common, and the ground is just begging to thaw. It's a steely-gray world, wet and raw with rare bursts of sunlight and color. A vast open world of small tarns, of lichens and moss and dwarf willows that grow in one hundred years no taller than a hands-breadth, no thicker than a pencil. In parts of the Sanderling's Canadian arctic, Musk-oxen ramble in small herds across these tundra plains, grazing willows and lichens; strange Pleistocene relics, "the smoldering embers of a fire that had refused to go out," as the biologist/painter George Sutton described these shaggy beasts. Wolves dig dens in sandy eskers, and jaegers—dark, hawk-like gulls—hunt lemmings and small birds with the relentless efficiency of arrows launched from crossbows.

Sanderlings touch down in this world, fresh from spring beaches of New Jersey and California, Hudson Bay and Saskatchewan—2,000-4,000 kilometers non-stop in two to three days—and are instantly at home. Their first imperative is to restore body reserves, fat and muscle burned in the long migration up from temperate latitudes. It is these reserves that will help produce eggs, the chief measure of success in the sanderling's world. To the human eye, food seems non-existent in this half-frozen tundra, but this bird is closer to the ground and far better initiated in the secrets of mud than we are. Here sanderlings find small worms and the larvae of midges and flies that will hatch in the infinite billions a few weeks later, with the first touches of warm sun. Slowly the birds regain weight. Internally they transform, losing flight muscle but gaining in gut and liver and other organs that process food. Courtship blossoms, with males fluttering slowly over the tundra like enormous butterflies, uttering odd frog-like calls over and over for minutes on end. Females, waiting below, appear satisfied with this; fertilized eggs emerge soon after, hidden in ground nests camouflaged among the lichens. By early July chicks hatch and almost immediately follow a parent out into the boundless arctic plain, tiny puffs of down on twig-like legs. They seem much too fragile to survive, all odds against them, but in reality are tough, resourceful, and alert to the faintest stir of insect life which in all its abundance will fuel their quick growth.

It is these birds—parent and chick—that I see a month or two later on the beaches of southern New England. Fresh from the world of dwarf willows and musk-oxen (I could be the first human they've seen—a humbling thought), they appear completely at home in their new habitat, gorging on mole crabs, building fat and muscle to power non-stop flights to South America. At dusk on clear August evenings with fresh northwest winds, I see them lift from the beach in restless flight, circling back in unison to feed briefly before jumping off again. Soon, I know, they will leave for good. Bermuda radars aligned to track bird migration show pulses of shorebirds moving high and fast over that island in late summer, at altitudes of one to two kilometers, traveling SSE. Sanderlings are among them. These are the ultra-marathoners among birds, burning twenty to thirty percent of their body mass in single flights of sixty to eighty hours, Cape Cod or New Jersey or the Carolinas to Venezuela or the Guianas or Colombia. They drop exhausted onto the mud beaches of northern South America, and sleep almost instantly, waking to feed voraciously in a few hours.

In a week or two they regain mass and strength. Some remain there all winter, roosting in small flocks along the edges of mangroves and moving out onto the hot wide beaches to feed at low tide. Others push south and east, flying another 3,000-4,000 kilometers over the rainforests of Brazil to the beaches of Patagonia, where tides of five to ten meters expose vast mudflats that teem with marine invertebrates. Who knows why some sanderlings travel on such distances, out of the tropics, while others stay. We do know that in temperate Patagonia they feed well and stay fat, alongside a few other arctic shorebirds, while southern right whales mate and give birth just a few hundred meters offshore. It's a rich world there. But by mid-April sanderlings are restless again, pushing north along many of the same routes that brought them south in fall. The Atlantic coast provides brief glimpses of them in May, especially in areas where food is abundant, but they are hurrying now, with the urgency of breeding upon them.

As long as mole crabs remain along my home beaches—and I suspect they won't become the next sushi delicacy—I'll expect sanderlings to return each summer, at least until the ice caps melt. Food is a powerful draw, especially once breeding is over. While it's reassuring to see those restless flocks reappear each July, reminding me that sand I once considered lifeless is not, my world feels small in the presence of these birds. But maybe less small now. Those small black eyes, searching the beach for flickers of crab antennae, have seen worlds I can reach at least in dreams: shiny-haired musk-oxen in arctic sun; Caribbean skies on moonlit nights, above the clouds; Patagonian mud.

Monarch
JASON LEE BROWN

Butterflies have returned to our oak tree four years running. Usually, they're here and long gone by now and Schooney's back to normal. Not this year. He backs my pick-up toward the barn and ignores my hand signals. He whips the tailgate inside and slams the truck in park, barely hitting the brakes. I let down the tailgate, the truck bed filled with fifty-pound feed sacks. He hops out and puts on his gloves. He's only twelve but he's been behind the wheel of everything on this farm and knows better. He hasn't said more than a couple words to me for a month or so, and when I ask him about his first little-league game, he just stacks the sacks next to the back wall of the barn like he doesn't hear me. He does this shit every year before the butterflies show up. He doesn't listen to me anymore and has stopped listening to my wife Rhonda long ago, and even if he did listen, all he'd hear is her bitching at me for drinking. He stacks like we're racing—three sacks to my one.

"Are you helping or not?" he says. He slams down a sack and wipes his forehead.

"I said I'd help and I'm helping." My back has been out for a week and I've been sleeping on a sheet of plywood.

I hear him mumble the word *shotgun*. He picks up another sack.

"Say it again," I say.

"You said you were getting me a *shotgun*," he says.

"You know how Rhonda feels about guns," I say, and when I hear the words in the air, I am as disgusted as he is.

"Who cares?" He turns away and slams down the sack.

I married Rhonda shortly after Schooney's mother died and though it's been five years, Schooney still hates her. He calls her RR. I have no idea why.

After we finish unloading the truck, our last chore of the day, I tell him to fetch me a beer from the cooler next to him before he sneaks off. Rhonda wants me to stop drinking altogether. She's always nagging so during our last argument I agreed to drink only at home.

"You know how RR feels about drinking," he says in his smart-ass tone that makes me want to laugh or choke him. He marches toward the shed next to the house. Normally, I'd beat his ass with my belt for smarting off but that would only make things worse. The first year after the accident, I didn't think Schooney was going to snap out of it. Didn't think I would. It's my fault his mother died. I wasn't in the car but right before the accident, we had a huge argument and I opened my mouth when I shouldn't have. She was gone, out the door, the last I ever saw her. Then it happened, one year after the accident, to the day. I watched my seven-year-old from the kitchen window. He puffed a cigarette, flicked the ashes, and lit the wick to a small rocket that shot out of a bottle and whistled somewhere over the cornfield and popped. He looked up at ten or so monarchs fluttering around his head. A large one landed in the grass next to his knee, its orange and black wings motionless. The rest rose into the oak tree. Several more butterflies dangled above him before landing. The heat that day had hit triple digits, and the monarchs must have stopped for shade. He yelled into the kitchen for me and Rhonda. Rhonda, pregnant and overdue, waddled out the back door. Butterflies had already painted a quarter of the tree orange and black. Just when I thought the monarchs would stop landing, more would fly out of nowhere and find a spot. It wasn't long before there was no green. Even the trunk was clustered. Schooney ran circles under the tree that breathed orange and black, his hands waving above his head. Butterflies fluttered in the air and landed again. For the first time since his mother's accident, he seemed happy. Two more weeks pass and still no butterflies. And I've had enough of this back-talking shit. Something's got to be done now or he's going to get worse. So this morning, I told him to finish his chores early then I walk by the shed after lunch, there he is in a chair, reading a magazine, feet propped up on his footlocker.

"I'll get to it," he says, before I can say anything.

"Finish chores and I'll take you into town."

"To shoot stick?" he says, making eye contact. I've been taking him to the tavern with me since his mother died, and he got so good at pool, I had to buy him his own stick.

"Nope," I say.

"Don't care," he says, his head behind the magazine.

"We can—"

"Close the door, please."

I tell him to just get in the truck. I don't want to talk about it in front of Rhonda.

"Why'd you buy the stick?" he says. "I never use it."

I don't want to tell him where we're going because I want to see his face light up when I pull into the gun store. I don't know how to trick him into the truck without physically tossing his ass in there.

"Get in the truck," I say in my I'm-not-messing-around voice. He studies me for a moment before he puts his head down and turns another page. I step toward him.

"What," he says and jumps up.

He must see it in my face. He sits back down and says he isn't going anywhere. If the butterflies are going to come, he's not missing them.

"You want a fucking shotgun or not?" I say.

On the way to town, he says he knows which shotgun he wants and how many shells he needs. He asks when he gets to hunt rabbits and pheasants and squirrels and he keeps asking questions without me answering, and we're there. I buy him the .410 and three boxes of shells. I plan on telling Rhonda that Schooney will probably shoot the gun for a while before tiring of it like he does with everything else. It'll probably hang on a gunrack in his playroom and he'll move on to something else. He wants to try everything but so far only nine-ball has kept his interest.

"Let's stop off at the tavern to celebrate," he says.

I should have kept my mouth shut when Rhonda asked why it mattered where I drank. The argument would have been over right there. She used to blame my drinking on losing my wife but now says so much time has passed I don't have any excuses. When Rhonda gets in her mood there's no stopping the argument. If she pauses and I don't talk, she will change the subject to something else she's been longing to bring up.

As I drive by the tavern I feel every bone in my body pulling toward the building so I turn the wheel and stop in the back of the lot.

"We'll just play pool," Schooney says. His fingers grip the door handle.

What could she say if I played pool with Schooney the rest of the night then drank beer when I got home?

"Should have brought our sticks," he says.

"We're not going in?" I say. Can't even shoot stick with my son

176

without permission. I let the truck idle around the building before going the wrong way through the drive-up. I don't want to see the owner Frona Lynn face-to-face or answer any of her questions. She sticks her head out the window and tries to look around Schooney at me. I look ahead.

"Where you been?" she says.

"Farming," I say.

Schooney leans forward and peeks through the window at the pool tables. Frona Lynn has been more of a mother to Schooney than Rhonda. At least he likes Frona Lynn. She hands a case and a bag of ice to Schooney and tells me not to be a stranger.

Rhonda is smoking a cigarette on the porch when I park the truck in the driveway. Schooney hops out and holds up the shotgun like a trophy. Rhonda starts yelling as soon as she sees it. She says she's only pissed because I didn't tell her first, which is bullshit. There's more to it than that. She follows me in the house to our bedroom. I take my twenty-gauge out of the gun case. I don't have the energy to deal with her. She won't let me finish anyway. Never does.

She says I do whatever I want, no matter what she says. But she's just trying to entice me into a bigger argument. She knows I want to say, if I did whatever I wanted, I'd be drinking at the bar while Schooney plays pool. I slide open the small gun-case drawer and grab a box of shells. Rhonda follows me through the bedroom and kitchen but stops at the back door.

Behind the Quonset hut, Schooney dumps my beer into the cooler. I smack the bag of ice on the concrete and wonder why everything has to be so dramatic with her. She never lets anything go. I cover the beer with the ice and close the lid. We stack empty beer cans into large triangles on top hay bales, and for the first time in months he's not preoccupied with butterflies. He doesn't even know he's smiling. I top off a triangle with a can.

We load our shotguns and blast the cans like a rigged carnival game, one stack after another, each shot echoing over the empty field. We trade guns for a few rounds then trade back. We restack and start keeping score to a game we are making up as we go along.

When Schooney's in high spirits, there's no stopping that kid. And we wouldn't have stopped if Rhonda didn't appear behind us, saying the fence behind the pig shed broke and there were two pigs missing. I tell him to find the pigs and I'll take a look at the fence.

"Every time," Schooney mumbles and he's right back to brooding. The gate behind the pig shed is bent forward, a broken hinge. I string bailing wire around the fencepost and the gate and tighten it with pliers for a temporary fix-up until I can weld the hinge back on. I'm tightening another wire when I hear screaming from the front yard. I take off to see Schooney by the tree with his arms above his head swatting at the air. "I knew it," he shouts. I jog closer and notice the swarm of butterflies hovering above him. He moves into the shade of the oak tree and the butterflies stick to the leaves above him. Rhonda and my four-year-old daughter Misty step off the porch and follow me. More monarchs clump together on the side of the tree. I wait for the rest but they never come. That doesn't seem to matter to Schooney. He reaches up like he wants to touch them but ruffles a branch instead, sending a cloud of butterflies into the air. A monarch lands on his arm and he cups it in his hand. The wings slowly open. Rhonda tells Misty to capture a butterfly and whisper a secret wish to it and the monarch will carry her wish to the Great Spirit. "Her wish will come true," Rhonda says, nodding, wanting Schooney to go along.

"Don't listen to her," Schooney says. He leans toward Misty. "Just more bullshit."

Glaring at Rhonda, Schooney raises the monarch to his lips and whispers something to it. Its wings touch as if taped together. He raises his arm and the monarch flutters two small loops in the air and floats away. She looks at me as if she can smell my beer breath and waits for me to say something. What can I say? He's right. She's bullying him and he doesn't want to go along, and I don't blame him. No one's going to tell him about those butterflies. Rhonda stomps back into the kitchen, pulling Misty by the arm. Schooney and I watch the butterflies dance in the air before picking a spot to land. As if someone turned on a faucet, heavy rain drenches us, but the sun won't stop shining. The butterflies cling to the trees. As fast as the downpour started, it stops, and a rainbow arches from behind the house toward town. I ask Schooney if he wants to go play pool after we chase down the pigs. He nods without taking his eyes off the monarchs that bask in the sun, still at first but eventually moving their wings to dry off.

On Migration and the Migratory Instinct
from the journals of HENRY D. THOREAU

Compiled by Jeffrey S. Cramer

23 MARCH 1856: I spend a considerable portion of my time observing the habits of the wild animals, my brute neighbors. By their various movements and migrations they fetch the year about to me. Very significant are the flight of geese and the migration of suckers, etc., etc.

18 APRIL 1852: I am serene and satisfied when the birds fly and the fishes swim as in fable, for the moral is not far off; when the migration of the goose is significant and has a moral to it; when the events of the day have a mythological character, and the most trivial is symbolical.

12 NOVEMBER 1853: I cannot but regard it as a kindness in those who have the steering of me that, by the want of pecuniary wealth, I have been nailed down to this my native region so long and steadily, and made to study and love this spot of earth more and more. What would signify in comparison a thin and diffused love and knowledge of the whole earth instead, got by wandering? The traveller's is but a barren and comfortless condition.

11 MARCH 1856: Only that travelling is good which reveals to me the value of home and enables me to enjoy it better.

23 APRIL 1852: Indians follow the buffaloes; trout, suckers, etc., follow the water-bugs, etc.; reptiles follow vegetation, insects, and worms; birds of prey, the fly-catchers, etc. Man follows all, and all follow the sun. The greater or less abundance of food determines migrations.

4 SEPTEMBER 1851: When you are starting away, leaving your more familiar fields, for a little adventure like a walk, you look at every object with a traveller's, or at least with historical, eyes; you pause on the first bridge, where an ordinary walk hardly commences, and begin to observe and moralize like a traveller.

27 JULY 1852: How cool and assuaging the thrush's note after the fever of the day! I doubt if they have anything so richly wild in Europe. So long a civilization must have banished it. It will only be heard in America, perchance, while our star is in the ascendant. I should be very much surprised if I were to hear in the strain of the nightingale such unexplored wildness and fertility, reaching to sundown, inciting to emigration.

17 MAY 1854: Observed a rill emptying in above the stone-heaps, and afterward saw where it ran out of June-berry Meadow, and I considered how surely it would have conducted me to the meadow, if I had traced it up. I was impressed as it were by the intelligence of the brook, which for ages in the wildest regions, before science is born, knows so well the level of the ground and through whatever woods or other obstacles finds its way. Who shall distinguish between the *law* by which a brook finds it river, the *instinct* [by which] a bird performs its migrations, and the *knowledge* by which a man steers his ship round the globe?

20 NOVEMBER 1857: The man who is often thinking that it is better to be somewhere else than where he is excommunicates himself.

11 MARCH 1856: When it was proposed to me to go abroad, rub off some rust, and *better my condition* in a worldly sense, I fear lest my life will lose some of its homeliness. If these fields and streams and woods, the phenomena of nature here, and the simple occupations of the inhabitants should cease to interest and inspire me, no culture or wealth would atone for the loss.

6 AUGUST 1851: A man must generally get away some hundreds or thousands of miles from home before he can be said to begin his travels. Why not begin his travels at home? Would he have to go far or look very closely to discover novelties? The traveller who, in this sense, pursues his travels at home, has the advantage at any rate of a long residence in the country to make his observations correct and profitable.

27 SEPTEMBER 1857: It is most natural, *i.e.* most in accordance with the natural phenomena, to suppose that North America was discovered from the northern part of the Eastern Continent, for a study of

the range of plants, birds, and quadrupeds points to a connection on that side. Many birds are common to the northern parts of both continents. Even the passenger pigeon has flown across there. And some European plants have been detected on the extreme northeastern coast and islands, which do not extend inland. Men in their migrations obey in the main the same law.

1 November 1858: Think of the consummate folly of attempting to go away from *here!* When the constant endeavor should be to get nearer and nearer *here* . . . How many things can you go away from? . . . Here is all the best and all the worst you can imagine. What more do you want? Bear here-away then! Foolish people imagine that what they imagine is somewhere else.

11 November 1851: To-day you may write a chapter on the advantages of travelling, and to-morrow you may write another chapter on the advantages of not travelling.

2 July 1851: A traveller! I love his title. A traveller is to be reverenced as such. His profession is the best symbol of our life. Going from— toward—; it is the history of every one of us.

notes on contributors

REBECCA ARONSON teaches writing at Northwest Missouri State University in Maryville, Missouri, where she also serves as co-editor for *The Laurel Review* and *GreenTower Press*. She has poems (recently or forthcoming) in *Tin House, Cimarron Review, The Cream City Review, Puerto del Sol, The Seattle Review, Phoebe*, and others.

RICK BASS is the author of more than twenty books of fiction and nonficiton. For complete notes, see interview on page 38.

JASON LEE BROWN teaches at Southern Illinois University in Carbondale. His work has appeared in the *Green Hills Literary Lantern, Spoon River Poetry Review, Margie, Concho River Review,* and *Pearl*, and his journalism recently won an award from the Illinois Press Association.

JEFFREY S. CRAMER is editor of the forthcoming: *What I Lived For: An Annotated Selection from Thoreau's Journals*. He is the Curator of Collections at the Thoreau Institute at Walden Woods, and has also edited *Walden: A Fully Annotated Edition* and *Thoreau on Freedom: Attending to an: Selected Writings of Henry David Thoreau*. Cramer's essays and other writings have appeared in *The Massachusetts Review, The Literary Review,* and *The Formalist*, among others, and have appeared in such collections as *Contemporary Literary Criticism* and *The Robert Frost Encyclopedia*.

ANN DARBY was the recipient of a 2004 Creative Writing Fellowship from the National Endowment for the Arts and is the author of the novel *The Orphan Game*, a *Los Angeles Times* bestseller. She has received the *Prairie Schooner* Reader's Choice Award, as well as the Bennett Cerf Prize for fiction, and her work has been nominated for the Pushcart and Henfield prizes. Her short fiction was listed among the "Recommended Stories" in the O. Henry Prize Stories 2005, and has appeared in *The Northwest Review, Prairie Schooner, The Manhattan Literary Review,* and *The Best of Story Quarterly*, among others. She lives in New York City and Hillsdale and is trying hard to learn to garden.

Born in Denver, Colorado, BURNS ELLISON grew up in Nebraska. He attended the University of Iowa Writers' Workshop in Iowa City in the 1960s. His most notable achievement from that period is a memoir published in *The Iowa Review* titled "The First Annual Nelson Algren Memorial Poker Game." In the 1990s, he got the graduate degree he didn't get from Iowa from the University of Colorado in Boulder. What he's done best in pursuing the literary life is acquiring those jobs that look good on the jacket of a book. These include working with disturbed kids in California, driving dog teams in Colorado, and being a shill in Nevada casinos. He now wants to get published the book that goes with the jacket.

KIMI FAXON is a founding editor of *Ecotone*. She received her MFA in creative nonfiction from the University of North Carolina Wilmington, where she currently teaches English composition and literature.

BARBARA FISHER's art combines both representational and abstract elements, hints at a narrative, and is illusionist while embracing abstract form and the physicality of paint. She received her BFA in painting from the University of Colorado and studied at San Francisco State University. She currently lives and works in Asheville, North Carolina. Her work was recently selected to be included in the upcoming publication, *The Best of North Carolina Artists and Artisans*, which will be published in 2006. She has also been chosen to serve as a panelist to select the recipients of the Ohio Arts Council's Individual Excellence Awards. Her website is www.barbarafisher.com.

RICHARD GARCIA is the author of *Rancho Notorious*, BOA Editions. His poems have recently appeared in *Sentence, The Notre Dame Review, Crazyhorse*, and *Ploughshares*. He is the recipient of a Pushcart prize and has a poem in *Best American Poetry 2005*. His next volume of poetry, *The Persistence of Objects*, is forthcoming from BOA in 2006.

ANDREW C. GOTTLIEB lives and writes in Seattle where he received his MFA from the University of Washington in 2000. His poetry chapbook, *Halflives*, has just been released from New Michigan Press and other work has appeared in many journals and magazines, including the *American Literary Review, Beloit Fiction Journal, Briar Cliff Review*, and *Poets & Writers*.

Ben Jones is a former editor of *The Adventure Library*. He has been awarded fellowships from the Vermont Studio Center and the National Endowment for the Humanities. His novel *The Rope Eater* was named one of the Top Ten Debuts of 2004 by the American Library Association. He prefers to live by rivers.

Sheila Kohler is the author of five novels: *The Perfect Place, The House on R Street, Cracks, Children of Pithiviers,* and *Crossways,* and three collections of short stories: *Miracles in America, One Girl,* and *Stories from Another World*. Kohler has been awarded the O. Henry, the Open Voice, and the Smart Family Foundation prizes and The Willa Cather Prize. *Cracks* was chosen by *Library Journal* and *Newsday* as one of the best books of 1999. Her work has appeared in *The Antioch Review, The American Voice, The Best American Short Stories 1999, Fiction, Five Points, New Letters, The Paris Review, Ploughshares,* and *The Yale Review,* among others.

Brian Laird lives in Tuscon, Arizona.

John Lane's books of prose include *Weed Time, Waist Deep in Black Water,* and *Chattooga*. He teaches at Wofford College in Spartanburg, SC, where for five years he has taught in a learning community linking freshman humanites and biology courses around the theme of water.

Alison Lester, mother of two, is a corporate communication coach and improvisational comedian living in Singapore. She has also lived in Beijing, Taipei, and Tokyo, where she worked as a freelance magazine writer and editor, and did voices for radio and television. A book of her stories has recently been accepted by Monsoon Books in Singapore.

Charlotte Matthews is the author of *Green Stars*. She also has two published chapbooks, *A Kind of Devotion* and *Biding Time*. Her poems have recently appeared in *Virginia Quarterly Review, Borderlands, Tar River Poetry, Sou'wester, The Mississippi Review, Spoon River Poetry Review, Meridian, Poet Lore,* and *Potomac Review*. She lives in Crozet, Virginia.

Sebastian Matthews is the author of the memoir *In My Father's Footsteps*. He has also co-edited, along with Stanley Plumly, *The Poetry*

Blues: Essays & Interviews of William Matthews and *Search Party: Collected Poems of William Matthews*, a recent finalist for the Pulitzer Prize. His poetry and prose have appeared in, among other places, *Atlantic Monthly, New England Review, Post Road, Seneca Review, Tin House* and *Virginia Quarterly Review*. Matthews lives with his wife and son in Asheville, North Carolina, where he teaches part-time at Warren Wilson College and edits *Rivendell*, a place-based literary journal. A chapbook of poems, *Coming to Flood*, is out with Hollyridge Press and a book of poems, *We Generous*, is forthcoming from Red Hen Press.

SARA PENNINGTON, a native of West Virginia and a graduate of Marshall University and Ohio University, lives in Tallahassee, Florida, where she continues to study and write poetry and is the editor of *The Southeast Review*. Her poems have recently appeared or are forthcoming in *The Greensboro Review, La Petite Zine, Nantahala, Kestrel*, and the anthology *Wild Sweet Notes II: More West Virginia Poetry*.

ALAN POOLE edits the *Birds of North America* life history series, now online and based at the Cornell Lab of Ornithology. He is the author of *Ospreys: An Unnatural History*. He divides his time between Ithaca, NY and the coast of Southeast Massachusetts, where he finds solace in salt marshes, a salad garden, and fly-fishing.

DAVID RIVARD's new collection, *Sugartown*, is forthcoming in early 2006 from Graywolf. His previous books include *Bewitched Playground* and *Wise Poison*, which won the James Laughlin Prize from the Academy of American Poets in 1996, and was a finalist for the Los Angeles Times Book Award. He teaches at Tufts University and in the MFA in Writing Program at Vermont College, and has had a long association with the Fine Arts Work Center in Provincetown.

ROBERT ROOT is the editor of the anthologies *Landscapes With Figures: The Nonfiction of Place* and, with Michael Steinberg, *The Fourth Genre: Contemporary Writers of/on Creative Nonfiction*. He is also the author of the critical study *E. B. White: The Emergence of an Essayist* and *Recovering Ruth: A Biographer's Tale*. His creative nonfiction works-in-progress are set along the Front Range of Colorado, the Hudson and Rhine Rivers, and the Erie Canal.

DEREK SHEFFIELD won the James Hearst Poetry Award judged by Li-Young Lee. In 2004, he received a Washington State Artist Trust Grant and David Wagoner selected nine of his poems to appear in a special section of the Fall 2004 *Poet Lore, Poets Introducing Poets.* New work is forthcoming in the *North American Review* and *Open Spaces.* He serves as the creative nonfiction editor for the *Seattle Review,* lives in an ecotone of pine forest and riparian meadow, and teaches writing and literature at Wenatchee Valley College.

JENNIFER SINOR teaches nonfiction prose at Utah State University. Her work has appeared in *Fourth Genre, Rosebud*, and *ISLE*, and she is currently co-editing a collection of essays that explore the relationship between place and academic identity. She lives with her husband and son on the edge of southeastern Idaho.

Originally from Connecticut, GRETCHEN STEELE is currently enrolled in the MFA program at Purdue University. This is her first publication.

MARGO TAMEZ (Lipan-Apache, Coahuiltec, Spanish Land Grant—Calaboz,Texas) is the author of *Alleys & Allies* and *Naked Wanting*. Two new collections are forthcoming in poetry and prose, *Raven Eye* and *The Daughter of Lightning,* both in 2006. Two recent anthologies in which her work appears are *Sister Nations: Native American Women Writers on Community* and *Dance the Guns to Silence: 100 Poems for Ken Saro-Wiwa.* She resides in Pullman, Washington, where she is on fellowship in the American Studies program.

MIKE WHITE grew up in Montreal and now lives in Salt Lake City. He is a doctoral candidate in creative writing at the University of Utah and serves as the poetry editor for *Quarterly West.* His recent work appears in journals including *Poetry, Margie, The Antioch Review*, and *The Iowa Review.*

PRAISE FOR **p o s t r o a D**

crazyhorse

Jawsmiths,
nightwalkers,
moonbirds:
Unite!

--from the Crazyhorse manifesto, 1960

Number 67 *Fiction* Maria Hummel's story of father and child bombed in Germany. Adam Schuitema's hero tries to stop a kidnapping. Anis Shivani's story wherein the grandfather just might be sincere. *Essays* Marianne Boruch on the thinky-thinky and the leapy-leapy of poetry. Richard Katrovas wonders how love leads inevitably to karate, and vice-versa. *Poetry* the scintillations and tintinnabulations of Eugénio de Andrade John Kinsella Adrian C. Louis Eva Saulitis Alexandra Teague G. C. Waldrep Marlys West Dara Wier and much more.

Subscriptions

$15
one year
(two issues)

$25
two years

$40
three years

$8.50
current issue

$5
sample
or back issue

Crazyhorse
Department of English
College of Charleston
66 George Street
Charleston, SC 29424
crazyhorse@cofc.edu
crazyhorse.cofc.edu

crazyhorse

Number 67   Spring 2005

MATTER
07: PATTERNS

a journal of literature, art, & movement

woodgrainswoodgrainswoodgrainswoodgrainswoodgrainswoodgrains

MATTER
07: Patterns

Featuring:
Fiction by Laura Pritchett, David Rozgonyi, Lesa Alison-Hastings
Non-fiction by Mark Hummel, Gary Wockner, Leslie Patterson
Poetry by Veronica Patterson, Jack Martin, Michael Salcman
and over seventy-five other contributors.

Published twice a year by Wolverine Farm Publishing *(501(c)3 status pending)*.
Subscription: $18 Year/Two Issues. Accepting submissions year-round.
Send to: Matter, PO BOX 814, Fort Collins, CO 80522.

www.wolverinefarmpublishing.org

THE JOURNAL

writing this good doesn't need a fancy name

---

the journal short story prize
1st prize $1000 and story publication
deadline may 1

william allen creative nonfiction prize
1st prize $500 and essay publication
deadline january 15

the osu press/the journal prize in poetry
1st prize $3000 and book publication
september postmark

the ohio state university prize in short fiction
1st prize $1500 and book publication
november postmark

for submission, subscription, contest and donation information:
http://english.osu.edu/journals/the_journal/

Ecotone welcomes unsolicited works of creative nonfiction, fiction, and poetry with a specific focus on place. Submissions are accepted between August 15 and April 30 only

Mail one prose piece and/or one to six poems at a time (mail genres separately). Prose should be typed double-spaced on one side of the page and be no longer than thirty pages. Poems should be typed either single- or double-spaced on one side of the page. Query letters should be sent for longer pieces. We have no preference in regards to names in headers or footers, or to staples or paper clips. Novel and memoir excerpts are acceptable if they are self-contained.

Please do not send multiple submissions in the same genre, and do not send another manuscript until you hear about the first. Include your full name and address on all envelopes. In general, address submissions to the editor in your genre. We generally follow *The Chicago Manual of Style*.

All manuscripts and correspondence regarding submissions should be accompanied by a self-addressed, stamped envelope (S.A.S.E.) for a response; no replies will be given by e-mail. Expect three months for a decision. We do not print previously published work, and we do not accept simultaneous submissions. We assume no responsibility for delay, loss, or damage. For more information about literary magazines, consult directories such as *NewPages*, *The Writer's Market*, and *The International Directory of Literary Magazines and Small Presses*.

Mail submissions to:
Ecotone
Genre Editor
Department of Creative Writing
University of North Carolina Wilmington
601 South College Road
Wilmington, NC 28403-3297

Ecotone does not accept electronic submissions.

Please visit us online at www.uncw.edu/ecotone.

E reimagining place
ECOTONE

Subscriptions:

Back issues: $9.95
One-year (two issues): $18
Two-years (four issues): $35
Three-years (six issues): $50

❐ send me a ____ -year subscription for $____.

Name: _____

Address: _____

_____

Phone number: _____

E-mail address: _____

Make check payable to *Ecotone* and mail to :

Ecotone
Department of Creative Writing
University of North Carolina Wilmington
601 South College Road
Wilmington, NC 28403-3297